SIN AND SOCIETY

AN ANALYSIS OF LATTER-DAY INIQUITY

BY

EDWARD ALSWORTH ROSS

PROFESSOR OF SOCIOLOGY IN THE UNIVERSITY OF WISCONSIN; AUTHOR OF
"SOCIAL CONTROL," "THE FOUNDATIONS OF SOCIOLOGY," ETC.

WITH A LETTER FROM
PRESIDENT ROOSEVELT

HARPER TORCHBOOKS
HARPER & ROW, PUBLISHERS
NEW YORK, EVANSTON, SAN FRANCISCO, LONDON

TO MY DEAR WIFE

ROSAMOND

THIS BOOK IS DEDICATED

INTRODUCTION
TO THE TORCHBOOK EDITION

ONE of the literary gems of the Progressive era—
and so recognized at the time of publication—is
this slender volume by the sociologist-reformer,
Edward Alsworth Ross entitled *Sin and Society:
An Analysis of Latter-Day Iniquity*. Ross's progressive inquiry into the moral and legal implica-
tions that inhered in the formation of corporate
imperialism, first published in 1907 and prefaced
with a letter of commendation by President Theodore Roosevelt, ranks alongside John Spargo's
The Bitter Cry of Children, Upton Sinclair's *The
Jungle*, and Robert Hunter's *Poverty* as a classic
example of the literature of protest fashioned by
the muckrakers in the first decade of the new century. *Sin and Society* is a unique blend of sociological theory and social reform; Ross named no
culprits nor did he, as did other muckrakers, write
an expose of a particular industry, problem, or
person. Along with other journalist-reformers of

the Progressive era, however, Ross was determined to use the printed word to enlighten public opinion and lead his readers in a crusade against the glaring inequities and injustices that dotted the social and economic landscape of the nation.

The enthusiasm generated by the publication of *Sin and Society* brought E. A. Ross to the height of his fame and influence and markedly influenced his future career. Ross had already established a formidable reputation for his scholarship and skill as a writer among that small group of people who established the foundations of American sociology at the turn of the century; the publication of *Sin and Society*, however, significantly broadened the spectrum of the sociologist-reformer's audience and dispelled any doubt that, in addition to his role as one of the nation's leading sociologists, here was a highly articulate and creative spokesman for the social reform of American life.

In his autobiography, *Seventy Years of It* (1937), Ross recognized the role of *Sin and Society* in bringing him national fame and the volume's classical quality as well. "It was wrought with such care," he wrote of *Sin and Society*, "that now, thirty years after, *I would not alter a com-*

ma." In a long and productive career, one that began prior to the Spanish-American War and came to an end only after World War II, E. A. Ross published more than two dozen books and some several hundred monographs and popular pieces. On many counts—as a literary tour de force as a hortatory call to the cause of reform, and as an exquisite amalgam of sociological and reformist thoughts—*Sin and Society* remains the crowning achievement of Ross's literary career.

The biographical aspects of Ross's early life—morning chores on the farm, education in a one-room schoolhouse, daily Bible reading and twice weekly prayer meetings at the church—correspond closely to the experiences of a generation of Americans who came to maturity in the towns and hamlets of the middle border in the decades immediately after the end of the Civil War. E. A. Ross was of Scots-Irish, Presbyterian stock. His father, William Carpenter Ross, an unsuccessful farmer, moved from one piece of land on the middle border to another in search for the main chance that never materialized. His mother, Rachel Ellsworth (Alsworth) was a schoolteacher in Marion, Iowa, in the 1840s and 1850s, a descendant of Thaddeus Dod[d], the revered minister-educator of Canonsburg, Pennsylvania, a bastion of Presbyterian piety and learning in the first half of the nineteenth century. Ross's parents were married in Marion in 1859. During the Civil War, the Rosses (and two children from a previous marriage by Rachel) left for Virden, a tiny town in Illinois a few miles east of the Mississippi River, where E. A. Ross was born on December 12, 1866.

Edward Ross's childhood was a fragmented and traumatic one, punctuated by a series of typical Scots-Irish perigrinations and climaxed by the early death of his parents. From Virden, the Rosses moved to Centralia, Kansas, and from Centralia to a farm near Davenport, Iowa. Rachel Ross died in 1874, when Edward was eight; his father died following the return of the family to Marion eighteen months later. In the fall of 1876, after being cared for by a bewildering number of paternal relatives, the youngster was given a foster home by John and Mary Beach on a farm on the outskirts of Marion. Well cared for by the Beaches, Ross remained with them until shortly after his fourteenth birthday, when he left to enroll in the prep department of Coe College in nearby Cedar Rapids.

The segmented relationships of his childhood years and the marginality he was forced to endure left their mark on the sensitive youngster. The precocious farmboy came away from his Iowa youth with a pronounced hostility toward those elements of society that enjoyed the luxury of wealth and privilege. As a sociologist, Ross focused largely on the sources of social order and the factors that produced social stability; as a reformer, he served as a spokesman for the aggrieved and the deprived. "It was a good thing for me," Ross wrote in summary of his youth on the middle border, "that, during my more sensitive years, I was a member of an element that was *looked down on;* it saved me...from the vice of snobbery. I have never cared to look down on *any one.*"

Enrollment at Coe marked the formal beginnings of a frenetic pursuit of fame and recognition that brought Ross to a full professorship at a major university within a single decade. The six-and-a-half-foot farmboy from Marion spent five years at Coe (1881–1886) and two as a member of the Fort Dodge Commercial Institute faculty (1886–1888). During these years he shed the fundamentalist Presbyterianism in which he had been reared, acquired a mastery of a half-dozen languages, and immersed himself deeply in a broad spectrum of nineteenth-century thought. While at Coe, Ross began to concern himself, too, with the myriad of inequities produced by the rapid industrialization of the nation's economy. In September 1888 Ross left Iowa for graduate study in languages, literature, and philology at the University of Berlin. A few months of central-European *Weltschmerz* convinced the ebullient Midwesterner to abandon Berlin for a *Wander-jahr* in Europe and eventual graduate study in the United States. He returned to America in December of 1889 and promptly enrolled in the graduate program in political economics under the nation's foremost social-gospel economist Richard T. Ely at Johns Hopkins University. In less than two years Ross earned his Ph.D. under Ely and prepared to enter the rapidly expanding world of the American university.

Two men, Ely and the sociologist Lester Frank Wand, served as the primary influences on Ross's early career and the blend of scholarship and re-form he wove into it. Ely served as a model for Ross of the academician-reformer, the paradigm

of the scholar who could both teach in the class-
room and influence public polity outside it. Of
even greater influence on Ross than Ely was
Ward, chief paleobotanist for the United States
Geological Survey and author of *Dynamic
Sociology* (1883), a tract Ross found to be an
exhilarating antidote to the Darwinian conserva-
tivism propounded in the writings of Herbert
Spencer and William Graham Sumner. As a con-
sequence of his relationship to Ward (whose niece
Ross married in 1892) and his own proclivities
as a social reformer, Ross moved from political
economy to sociology by the end of the decade.
Both Ely and Ward confirmed a number of con-
clusions Ross had already come to and which he
later incorporated into his writings generally and
into *Sin and Society* in particular: a disdain of
ironclad economic or social laws and a rejection
of the determinism inherent in the evolutionary
thought of Spencer and Sumner, their survival-
of-the-fit political philosophy, their laissez-faire
definition of the state, and their denigration of the
efficacy of social reform. All three—Ward, Ely,
and Ross—proposed instead an alteration of the
nation's laws and institutions and a positive role
for the state in order to meet the requirements of

social and economic change. As turn-of-the-century Progressives, they would buttress the positive role of government and stress the principle of cooperation in society in order to preserve the free and equitable competition of its individual members.

Changes in the structure and the purposes of the American university by the 1890s with emphasis on research, graduate teaching, and publication opened vast opportunities for a man of Ross's mobile temperament and scholarly gifts. After one year at Indiana University (1891–1893), Ross accepted a full professorship at the newly founded Stanford University in Palo Alto, California. Once on the West Coast the scholar-reformer perfected a routine that would remain with him for the remainder of his life, a role that combined a prolific blend of scholarly research and publication on one hand, and a torrent of popular commentary in print and in public lectures on current issues on the other. The economist-turned-sociologist achieved lasting fame among sociologists here and abroad with the publication of his magnum opus, *Social Control: A Survey of the Foundations of Order*

(1901). *The Foundations of Sociology* (1905), largely a collection of monographs on sociological theory and *Social Psychology* (1908), the first American text on the subject, further reinforced Ross's scholarly reputation. These volumes, along with the popular pieces he contributed to *The Arena, The Independent, The Outlook,* and other magazines, stamped Ross as an important spokesman on the social and economic issues of the day.

Ultimately, the Populist-Progressive texture of Ross's public pronouncements led to his dismissal from Stanford and a nationwide controversy over the question of whether academic freedom had been violated by the university's action. Ross lost his post at Stanford because Jane Lathrop Stanford, the beneficent, yet highly authoritarian widow of the university's founder could not tolerate a scholar who roundly condemned the ethics and the social irresponsibility of the business community, who urged more effective labor unions and farm organizations, the public ownership of municipal transportation, Free Silver and the election of William Jennings Bryan in 1896, and who spoke out sharply against the continued immigration of the Japanese to the

West Coast. The ouster of Ross and the furor caused by this action, as well as the subsequent resignation of seven others from the Stanford faculty (including Arthur O. Lovejoy), brought disgrace to the university and an added aura of martyrdom to Ross's already considerable reputation. Ross survived the dismissal and even flourished as a result of it for two reasons: because of his impeccable credentials as a scholar and because a Progressive spirit was beginning to stir in the land. In February 1901 Ross went to the University of Nebraska where we was offered a full professorship in sociology by the chancellor, E. Benjamin Andrews, who was, like Ross, an academic victim of the antisilver forces of 1896. Five years later Ross left Nebraska to join Ely, John R. Commons, and the remainder of the academic task force for progressivism at the University of Wisconsin. "From 1903 on," Ross writes of the years in which *Sin and Society* was fashioned, "the Hanna-Aldrich-Quayice sheet was retreating and the sleet was giving way to sunshine for us champions of the social welfare."

Sin and Society grew out of series of lectures given by Ross just after the turn of the century and incorporated later into six articles and published in the *Atlantic Monthly* between 1905 and 1907. Neither Ross nor Bliss Perry, the editor at the *Atlantic*, were quite prepared for the wildly enthusiastic reception accorded the essays when they appeared in print. One reader, after reading the first of the series, suggested "that the publishers consider an edition of some millions of copies." Ross soon began to shop around for a publisher and a suitable title for the collection. Among those considered and discarded were *The New Uprightness* and *The Common Peril*. Ross finally signed a contract with the Houghton Mifflin Company (publishers of the *Atlantic*) for *Smokeless Sin: An Analysis of Latter-Day Iniquity*, a title that, in his opinion, conveyed the notion that "wrongdoing of the modern type inflicts harm, is hard to locate, outwardly offensive, not maladorous, remote from the harm it causes, indifferent in its choice of victim and passionless in execution." Despite this logic, Ross had the good sense to listen to his friend Theodore Roosevelt and abandon *Smokeless Sin* for *Sin and Society*.

The underlying theme of the tract is trumpeted by Ross in his opening paragraph: "Modern sin," the sociologist tells his readers, "takes its character from the mutualism of our time"; antisocial behavior grows out of and, therefore, must be redefined to conform to the emerging collectivism of an urban-industrial order ("society") that is in the process of destroying and that will ultimately replace the individualistic agrarian-commercial economy ("community") of an earlier era. Leaning heavily on the distinctions he and other sociologists (especially, in this particular chapter, the notions of the French sociologist, Emile Durkheim) had drawn between "community" and "society," Ross made it clear throughout the volume that the nation's primary need was to update its moral notions and legal sanctions in order to meet the requirements of the social and economic changes coming into the fabric of the American nation. "Mutualism," the term employed by Ross to explain to his lay audience the functional interdependence of individuals, institutions, and processes of a corporate society, has established both the context and the opportunity for modern wrongdoing. "The water main is my well, the trolley car my carriage, the banker's safe my old stocking, the policeman's billy my fist.... I rely upon others to look after my drains, invest my savings, nurse my sick and teach my children." Over and over again Ross hammered home one of the fundamental premises of his generation of sociologists, the notion that *community* was being replaced by *society*, that the relative simplicity of the economic system and the face-to-face relationships of an earlier era were about to give way to the complexity and the impersonality of the twentieth century. The illustrations offered by Ross were many: "I let the meat trust butcher my pig, the oil trust mould my cancles, the sugar trust boil my sorghum, the coal trust chop my wood, the barb wire company split my rails." As Woodrow Wilson noted in 1912, the American people "are in the presence of a new organization of society." In his letter of introduction to *Sin and Society*, Theodore Roosevelt was even more succinct: "You show," he wrote to Ross, "that the worst evils we have to combat have inevitably evolved along with the evolution of society itself, and that the perspective of conduct must change from age to age."

Ross clearly delineated the singular character of modern wrongdoing: it is novel and subtle and therefore hard to detect; it is also impersonal, dangerous for its victims and for the nation, and highly lucrative for its practitioners. "Latter-day

crime...rarely calls for the spilling of blood,"
Ross told his readers. "What an abyss between
the knife-play of brawlers and the law-defying
neglect to fence dangerous machinery in a mill,
or to furnish cars with safety couplers!" In highly
purple prose Ross drew a distinction between the
popular image of the criminal type and his true-
to-life counterpart: "The stealings and slayings
that lurk in the complexities of our social relations
are not needs of the dive, the dark alley, the lonely
road, and the midnight hour. They require no
nocturnal prowlings with muffled step and bated
breath, no weapon or offer of violence. Unlike the
old-time villain, the latter-day malefactor does
not wear a slouch hat and a comforter, breathe
forth curses and an odor of gin." The new criminal element in the nation is the unscrupulous
businessman; "Fagin and Bill Sykes and Simon
Legree are vanishing types."

Unfortunately, Ross explained, the public is
rarely able to identify the true enemies of society
or to gauge the full extent of the harm these men
inflict on the nation. Committed to an outmoded
moral code, laymen tend to assess wrongdoers on
the basis of traditional, yet highly irrelevant
criteria: on the wickedness of their characters and

degree of violence they employ, their social manners and their educational level, and their standing in the community. These indexes of deviant behavior will no longer suffice. The undiscerning fail to see "that boodling is treason, that blackmail is piracy, that embezzlement is theft, that speculation is gambling, that tax-dodging is larceny, that railroad discrimination is treachery, that the factory labor of children is slavery, that deleterious adulteration is murder." Ross pinpointed the changes in American society that had altered both the definition and the opportunity for wrongdoing: "The growth of credit institutions, the spread of fiduciary relations, the enmeshing of industry in law, the interlacing of government and business, the multiplication of boards and inspectors." Under these conditions, Ross concluded, "the old righteousness it not enough" and urged, therefore, "an annual supplement to the Decalogue." Otherwise, "how idle to intone the old litanies!"

The antibusiness animus that pervades *Sin and Society* reaches its climax in Ross's discussion of "the criminaloid," who is defined by Ross as the businessman who manages to exploit every development in the economy for his own profit through practices against which society has not yet learned to protect itself. Ross described the activities of the *criminaloid* thusly: "Surpass as their misdeeds may in meanness and cruelty, there has not yet been time enough to store up strong emotion about them; and so the sight of them does not let loose the flood of wrath and abhorrence that rushes down upon the long-attainted sins." Careful to stay within the letter of the law, these men do more harm to the country than thieves or murderers: while the latter earns his livelihood "menacing our purses," the *criminaloid* tampers with "the ideals" of the nation. Ross offered numerous examples of the *criminaloid*: trustees who speculate with a corporation's assets; banks who borrow from their depositors' savings; and publishers who bribe school officials in order to obtain textbook adoptions. Warning his readers against the *criminaloid's* pretense of respectability (their "protective mimicry of the good" through a facade of "religiosity," "respectability," "ostentatious philanthropy," and "spread-eagle patriotism") Ross would have Progressives "run [the *criminaloid*] to earth and brand him, as long ago pirate and traitor were branded."

Sin and Society closes with a plea to the American people and, particularly, the business community to abide by what Ross called "the rules of the game"—adherence to an economic system that would enable individuals to compete fairly with one another for material gain. Like most Progressives, Ross had no quarrel with the basic tenets of American capitalism—the sanctity of private property, economic individualism, and the competitive system. But, like many of them, specifically, Woodrow Wilson, Ross wanted to equalize "the race of life," to provide continued opportunity for the "man on the make." Two factors, the close of the frontier and the concentration of industry, led Ross to feel that perhaps the opportunities for the aspiring individual so characteristic of the previous century might be coming to an end. He consequently urged that the government remain impartial in the conflict of interests between classes and interests. "Tampering with the rules of the game finally brings the game itself into discredit," he warned. Ross's was a plea for reform in order to ward off revolution, for the nation to accept a capitalistic system he called "transfigured individualism" in order to prevent radicals from altering our form of economy and government in a more basic and unsatisfactory way. Should big business fail to accede to social and economic reform, "there is sure to form a body of tangent opinion denying everything that capitalism affirms and affirming everything that capitalism denies. The Nemesis of treating private property, freedom of enterprise, and corporate undertaking as instruments of *private gain* rather than of *public welfare*," he warned, "is the root-and-branch man who urges us to escape the Unendurable by taking refuge in the Impossible."

The success of *Sin and Society* as a Progressive tract rested on several qualities. On one hand, the book's inner fire—its biblical rhetoric and hortatory texture—had great appeal for a generation of readers reared on the moralistic fare contained in the McGuffey readers, Sunday schools, and the weekly sermons of small-town, Protestant divines. At the same time the sociologist offered his readers a daringly relativist conceptualization of social morality, one that would enable Progressives to identify the wrongdoers in their midst and provide an adequate rationale for legislative and legal sanctions to deal with them and their transgressions. *Sin and Society* satisfied the Progressives' need to be both virtuous as well as efficient.

Sin and Society had yet other attributes: Without naming names, thereby enabling each reader to escape the onus of the author's censure, Ross made it illuminatingly clear how to identify evil and bring to it the condemnation it deserved. *Sin and Society* enabled Progressives to take the moral initiative from the conservatives who had for so many decades enjoyed a monopoly of public support in their efforts to label as subversive any regulation of the economy or industry on behalf of labor, the farmer, or the consumer. And yet, despite the white heat of Ross's rage against the *criminaloid*, his tract was pervaded by a sense of optimism and moderation. As a good Progressive, Ross did not feel that our economic system needed any major surgery, any radical alteration of its basic rules. Ross's call for a "transfigured individualism," for businessmen to abide by "the rules of the game" reflected more of a confidence in the essential soundness of the capitalistic enterprise than a desire to scuttle it. As in *Social Control,* Ross sought to find a balance between the requirements of individual freedom and the need for social stability and justice.

The response to the publication of *Sin and*

Society gratified the book's author and publisher. Within a year of publication, more than 1,200 copies of *Sin and Society* had been sold and by 1942, the year Houghton Mifflin melted down the plates, the volume had gone through seventeen printings with sales totaling 8,817. For good reason the publishers could inform Ross that this was "a most satisfactory showing for a book of [this] type."

"I *love you* Professor Ross for the moral grandeur of your ethical daring," wrote one reader; another informed the author that the book would be used "as ammunition for better civic conditions" in his home town. One college president called it "the greatest thing I have seen in print; a Cleveland banker bought an extra copy to lend to his friends while a California editor presented copies of *Sin and Society* to his friends as gifts for Christmas. Most complimentary was a request from William Jennings Bryan for permission to publish the work in a cheaper, paperback edition for the readers of *The Commoner*. From Stephen W. Stookey, Dean at Coe College and a former classmate of Ross's, came a touching and prophetic letter: "I...read every word of [*Sin and Society*] as it came out in the magazine, and then I began at the beginning of the book and read it through, part of it to my family. You...are only just beginning your most influential career," Stookey concluded. "I look forward for your continued development in power and influence for twenty-five years to come."

The influence of *Sin and Society* transcended its immediate impact on Progressive thought and morale. Beneath the book's moralistic rhetoric, *Sin and Society* contained a sophisticated view of the emerging corporate economy and the transformation in social norms and legal sanction that would be required in order to preserve a stable and equitable social and economic order.

Sin and Society also helped advance a pragmatic and melioristic conception of jurisprudence–the notion that the law grows out of social and economic realities and that it can be used as an instrument to improve them. Ross acquired a naturalistic view of the law through his readings in nineteenth-century historical jurisprudence and a familiarity with the works of Rudolph von Ihering on the Continent, Sir Henry Maine in England, and Oliver Wendell Holmes, Jr., at home. These men led Ross, as did his own work on *Social Control*, to accept a fully naturalistic view of the law and to understand the law as Holmes described it, as growing out of "life," not "logic." Like Holmes, Ross would alter the law to meet the alterations taking place in the marketplace and in accordance with the needs and the demands of the majority of the nation. Both men attacked the inviolability of the counts and the sacrosanct character of judicial decisions. "Our law officers," *Sin and Society* announced in the spirit of Holmes, "are not socially and politically ...distinct from the people. Their individuality is not so completely merged in their function.... We dream that we live under a government of laws; we are actually under a government of men."

Sin and Society bridged the gap between the naturalistic jurisprudence of Holmes and the more avowedly reformist sociological jurisprudence as practiced by Louis Dembitz Brandeis and taught at the law schools of Nebraska, Chicago, and Harvard by Roscoe Pound. *Sin and Society,* as did Brandeis in his famous sociological brief in *Muller v. Oregon* (asking the Supreme Court to uphold a state law limiting the working hours of female factory workers) posits the notion that the law, growing out of social conditions, can be used to improve them. Ross's relationship to and influence on Pound was a more explicit one. "You have set me in the path the world is moving in," wrote Pound, soon to become the nation's foremost exponent of sociological jurisprudence, to Ross shortly after the sociologist left Nebraska for Wisconsin. All three men—Ross, Brandeis, and Pound—opposed the formalistic and artificial conceptions developed by nineteenth-century jurists in order to justify economic rapacity and social inequity. In harmony with *Sin and Society* they would judge legal doctrines on the basis of their humanity and justice rather than on the basis of their legal consistency. As a disciple of Ross, Pound taught his students, "in the separation of jurisprudence from sociology there is stagnation and that law has been greatly deficient in the past by virtue of its divorcement from social ends."

As a sociological tract *Sin and Society* anticipated the "cultural lag" theory developed with greater sophistication in the 1920s by the sociologist William Fielding Ogburn. In essence, Ross defined the principal problem of the nation as growing out of a disparity between the accelerated rate of economic and technological change, what Ogburn called the material culture, and the more slowly changing legal, political, and ethical norms, Ogburn's superorganic culture. Ross and later Ogburn saw society as an organic whole and wanted to reduce moral confusion and social pathology by maintaining a functional harmony between the nation's material culture and its nonmaterial one.

Ross's successful venture in popularizing sociological ideas permanently altered his career line, although tendencies toward becoming a publicist were discernible prior to the publication of *Sin and Society*. After 1907 Ross began more and more to neglect the serious monograph for the popular essay, to publish easily-written social commentary rather than to engage in the more taxing and less lucrative research required for the scholarly publication. After *Sin and Society* appeared, Ross received more requests from publishers than he could possibly fulfill and his fees rose from $50, what the *Atlantic* paid for each of the *Sin and Society* articles, to $250 and, on occasion, much more. The demand for these popular pieces, in addition to his success on the lecture circuit, opened up a full parallel career to Ross, that of essayist, social critic, and commentator to the nation at large. Ross spent the remainder of his life cultivating this facet of his career while still maintaining his post as sociologist-in-residence at the University of Wisconsin.

In 1910 Ross left for China and launched himself as a reporter to the nation on social conditions abroad. These sociological travelogues, beginning with *The Changing Chinese* (1911) and *South of Panama* (1914), account for one-third of Ross's total publications. In 1917 Ross was sent to Russia by Josiah Strong's American Institute for Social Service to assess the revolution there. Ross responded by publishing three books that were, on the whole, favorable in attitude toward the Bolshevik revolution and the Soviet Union: *Russia in Upheaval* (1917), *The Russian Bolshevik Revolution* (1921), and *The Russian Soviet Republic* (1923). Various aspects of revolution and social change abroad were further explored by Ross in *The Social Revolution in Mexico* (1923) and in *World Drift* (1928). Ross brought to all these reports a perceptive eye for significant economic and social trends, as well as a literary style at once brilliant and lucid.

As a reformer on the domestic scene, Ross maintained a liberal posture throughout his career, albeit that posture was colored, and at times appallingly so, by a syndrome of nativistic attitudes. A warmed-over and unsuccessful effort to duplicate *Sin and Society* appeared in 1910 entitled *Latter Day Sinners and Saints*. Other books advocating social reform include *Changing America* (1909 and 1912), *The Social Trend* (1922), and *Roads to Social Peace* (1924). Ross's nativism included a strident hostility toward the "new immigration" and a desire to restrict their immigration into the United States *(The Old World in the New* [1914]), a commitment to prohibition and racist engenics *(The Social Trend* [1922]), and a concern for world population trends *(Standing Room Only?* [1927]). Ross shed his nativism in the 1930s, a period in which he solidly supported the New Deal and other liberal movements of the depression decade. Ross spent the last decades of his life as an outspoken and fearless champion of the rights of the individual in American society — defending civil liberties (freedom of speech and the press) and academic freedom. Appropriately, Ross served from 1940 to 1950 as national chairman of the American

Civil Liberties Union.

Ross died in Madison, Wisconsin, in his eighty-fifth year on July 22, 1951. If his reputation as a scholarly figure in American sociology has declined since his death, this is largely of Ross's own doing. Had he eschewed the lecture platform and the popular essay, undoubtedly his scholarly contribution to American sociology would have been a more durable one. But this was not his way or his purpose. The purpose of sociology, in Ross's view, was the improvement of society, and he needed to reach as wide an audience as he could. As Ross put it, "[I] have uttered with all the 'bang' at [my] command *everything* [I] *felt sure of.*" Social reform, in Ross's view transcended the need for refinement of "scope and method." In this sense applying the fruits of sociological research for the purpose of elevating the moral and legal sanctions of the American nation, *Sin and Society* was Ross's finest hour.

PREFACE

THIS book deals with sin, but it does not entreat the sinner to mend his ways. It seeks to influence no one in his conduct. It does seek to influence men *in their attitude toward the conduct of others*. Its exhortation is not *Be good*, but *Be rational*. To modify conduct one touches the heart. To modify the judgments on conduct one speaks to the intellect. The latter is the method of this book. Its aim is to enlighten rather than to move.

In praising or blaming each of us exerts a power over his fellows. When the praises or blames of many men run together, they become a torrent no one can withstand. Why let this moral power run to waste? Why not use this public opinion to protect our dearest possessions?

In its reactions against wrong-doing the public is childishly naïve and sentimental. It is content with the surface look of things. It lays emphasis where emphasis was laid centuries ago. It beholds sin in a false perspective, seeing peccadillos as crimes, and crimes as peccadillos. It never occurs to the public that sin evolves along with society, and that the perspective in which it is necessary to view misconduct changes from age to age. Hence, in to-day's warfare on sin, the reactions of the public are about as serviceable as gongs and stink-pots in a modern battle. Rationalize public opinion; modernize it and bring it abreast of latter-day sin ; make the blame of the many into a flaming sword guarding the sacred interests of society — such is the lesson this little book seeks to impress.

EDWARD ALSWORTH ROSS.

MADISON, WIS., September, 1907.

A LETTER

OYSTER BAY, N. Y.,
September 19, 1907.

My dear Professor Ross:

It was to Justice Holmes that I owed the pleasure and profit of reading your book on Social Control. The Justice spoke of it to me as one of the strongest and most striking presentations of the subject he had ever seen. I got it at once and was deeply interested in it. Since then I have read whatever you have written. I have been particularly pleased with the essays which, as you tell me, you are now to publish in permanent form. You define "sin" as conduct that harms another in contradistinction to "vice," by which we mean practices that harm one's self; and you attack as they should be attacked the men who at the present day do more harm to the body politic by their sinning than all others. With almost all that you write I am in full and hearty sympathy. As you well say, if a ring is to be put in the snout of the greedy strong, only organized society can do it. You war against the vast iniquities in modern business, finance, politics, journalism, due to the ineffectiveness of public opinion in coping with the dominant types of wrong-doing in a huge, rich, highly complex industrial civilization like ours. You show that the worst evils we have to combat have inevitably evolved along with the evolution of society itself, and that the perspective of conduct must change from age to age, so that our moral judgment may be recast in order more effectively to hold to account the really dangerous foes of our present civilization. You do not confine yourself to mere destructive criticism. Your plea is for courage, for uprightness, for far-seeing sanity, for active constructive work. There is no reason why we should feel despondent over the outlook of modern civilization, but there is every reason why we should be fully alert to the dangers ahead. Modern society has developed to a point where there is real cause for alarm lest we shall go the way of so many ancient communities, where the state was brought to ruin because politics became the mere struggle of class against class. Your book is emphatically an appeal to the general sense of right as opposed to mere class interest. As you put it, the danger is as great if the law is twisted

to be an instrument of the greed of one class as
if it is twisted to be an instrument of the vengefulness of another. You reject that most mischievous of socialist theses, viz. : that progress
is to be secured by the strife of classes. You
insist, as all healthy-minded patriots should insist, that public opinion, if only sufficiently en-
lightened and aroused, is equal to the necessary
regenerative tasks and can yet dominate the
future. Your book is wholesome and sane and
I trust that its influence will be widespread.

Sincerely yours,

Theodore Roosevelt

CONTENTS

I

NEW VARIETIES OF SIN

NEW VARIETIES OF SIN

THE sinful heart is ever the same, but sin changes its quality as society develops. Modern sin takes its character from the mutualism of our time. Under our present manner of living, how many of my vital interests I must intrust to others! Nowadays the water main is my well, the trolley car my carriage, the banker's safe my old stocking, the policeman's billy my fist. My own eyes and nose and judgment defer to the inspector of food, or drugs, or gas, or factories, or tenements, or insurance companies. I rely upon others to look after my drains, invest my savings, nurse my sick, and teach my children. I let the meat trust butcher my pig, the oil trust mould my candles, the sugar trust boil my sorghum, the coal trust chop my wood, the barb wire company split my rails.

But this spread-out manner of life lays

snares for the weak and opens doors to the wicked. Interdependence puts us, as it were, at one another's mercy, and so ushers in a multitude of new forms of wrong-doing. The practice of mutualism has always worked this way. Most sin is prey-ing, and every new social relation begets its cannibalism. No one will " make the ephah small " or "falsify the balances " un-til there is buying and selling, " withhold the pledge " until there is loaning, " keep back the hire of the laborers" until there is a wage system, " justify the wicked for a reward" until men submit their disputes to a judge. The rise of the state makes possi-ble counterfeiting, smuggling, peculation, and treason. Commerce tempts the pirate, the forger, and the embezzler. Every new fiduciary relation is a fresh opportunity for breach of trust. To-day the factory system makes it possible to work children to death on the double-quick, speculative building gives the jerry-builder his chance, long-

range investment spawns the get-rich-
quick concern, and the trust movement
opens the door to the bubble promoter.

The springs of the older sin seem to be
drying up. Our forced-draught pace re-
lieves us of the superabundance of energy
that demands an explosive outlet. Spasms
of violent feeling go with a sluggish habit
of life, and are as out of place to-day as are
the hard-drinking habits of our Saxon an-
cestors. We are too busy to give rein to
spite. The stresses and lures of civilized
life leave slender margin for the gratifica-
tion of animosities. In quiet, side-tracked
communities there is still much old-fashioned hatred, leading to personal clash, but
elsewhere the cherishing of malice is felt
to be an expensive luxury. Moreover, brutality, lust, and cruelty are on the wane.
In this country, it is true, statistics show
a widening torrent of bloody crime, but
the cause is the weakening of law rather
than an excess of bile. Other civilized peo-

ples seem to be turning away from the sins of passion.

The darling sins that are blackening the face of our time are incidental to the ruthless pursuit of private ends, and hence quite "without prejudice." The victims are used or sacrificed not at all from personal ill-will, but because they can serve as pawns in somebody's little game. Like the wayfarers run down by the automobilist, they are offered up to the God of Speed. The essence of the wrongs that infest our articulated society is betrayal rather than aggression. Having perforce to build men of willow into a social fabric that calls for oak, we see on all hands monstrous treacheries, — adulterators, peculators, boodlers, grafters, violating the trust others have placed in them. The little finger of Chicane has come to be thicker than the loins of Violence.

The sinister opportunities presented in this webbed social life have been seized unhesitatingly, because such treasons have not yet become infamous. The man who picks pockets with a railway rebate, murders with an adulterant instead of a bludgeon, burglarizes with a "rake-off" instead of a jimmy, cheats with a company prospectus instead of a deck of cards, or scuttles his town instead of his ship, does not feel on his brow the brand of a malefactor. The shedder of blood, the oppressor of the widow and the fatherless, long ago became odious, but latter-day treacheries fly no skull-and-crossbones flag at the masthead. The qualities which differentiate them from primitive sin and procure them such indulgence may be clearly defined.

MODERN SIN IS NOT SUPERFICIALLY REPULSIVE

To-day the sacrifice of life incidental to quick success rarely calls for the actual spilling of blood. How decent are the pale slayings of the quack, the adulterator, and

the purveyor of polluted water, compared
with the red slayings of the vulgar bandit
or assassin! Even if there is blood-letting,
the long-range, tentacular nature of modern homicide eliminates all personal colli-
sion. What an abyss between the knife-
play of brawlers and the law-defying neglect
to fence dangerous machinery in a mill,
or to furnish cars with safety couplers!
The providing of unsuspecting passengers
with "cork" life-preservers secretly loaded
with bars of iron to make up for their
deficiency in weight of cork, is spiritually
akin to the treachery of Joab, who, taking
Amasa by the beard "to kiss him," smote
Amasa "in the fifth rib;" but it wears a
very different aspect. The current methods
of annexing the property of others are
characterized by a pleasing indirectness
and refinement. The furtive, apprehensive
manner of the till-tapper or the porch-
climber would jar disagreeably upon the
tax-dodger "swearing off" his property,

he causes. Upon his gentlemanly presence the eventual blood and tears do not obtrude themselves.

This is why good, kindly men let the wheels of commerce and of industry redden and redden, rather than pare or lose their dividend. This is why our railroads yearly injure one employee in twenty-six, and we look in vain for that promised "day of the Lord" that "will make a man more precious than fine gold."

MODERN SINS ARE IMPERSONAL

The covenant breaker, the suborned witness, the corrupt judge, the oppressor of the fatherless, — the old-fashioned sinner, in short, — knows his victim, must hearken, perhaps, to bitter upbraidings. But the tropical belt of sin we are sweeping into is largely impersonal. Our iniquity is wireless, and we know not whose withers are wrung by it. The hurt passes into that vague mass, the "public," and is there lost to view. Hence it does not take a Borgia to knead "chalk and alum and plaster" into the loaf, seeing one cannot know just who will eat that loaf, or what gripe it will give him. The purveyor of spurious life-preservers need not be a Cain. The owner of rotten tenement houses, whose "pull" enables him to ignore the orders of the health department, foredooms babies, it is true, but for all that he is no Herod.

Often there are no victims. If the crazy hulk sent out for "just one more trip" meets with fair weather, all is well. If no fire breaks out in the theatre, the sham "emergency exits" are blameless. The corrupt inspector who O. K.'s low-grade kerosene is chancing it, that is all. Many sins, in fact, simply augment risk. Evil does not dog their footsteps with relentless and heart-shaking certainty. When the catastrophe does come, the sinner salves his conscience by blasphemously calling it an "accident" or an "act of God."

Still more impersonal is sin when the immediate harm touches beneficent institutions rather than individuals, when, following his vein of private profit, the sinner drives a gallery under some pillar upholding our civilization. The blackguarding editor is really undermining the freedom of the press. The policy kings and saloon keepers, who get out to the polls the last vote of the vicious and criminal classes, are sapping manhood suffrage. Striking engineers who spitefully desert passenger trains in mid-career are jeopardizing the right of a man to work only when he pleases. The real victim of a lynching mob is not the malefactor, but the law-abiding spirit. School-board grafters who blackmail applicants for a teacher's position are stabbing the free public school. The corrupt bosses and "combines" are murdering representative government. The perpetrators of election frauds unwittingly assail the institution of the ballot.

Rarely, however, are such transgressions abominated as are offenses against persons.

Because of the special qualities of the Newer Unrighteousness, because these devastating latter-day wrongs, being comely of look, do not advertise their vileness, and are without the ulcerous hag-visage of the primitive sins, it is possible for iniquity to flourish greatly, even while men are getting better. Briber and boodler and grafter are often "good men," judged by the old tests, and would have passed for virtuous in the American community of seventy years ago. Among the chiefest sinners are now enrolled men who are pure and kindhearted, loving in their families, faithful to their friends, and generous to the needy.

One might suppose that an exasperated public would sternly castigate these modern sins. But the fact is, the very qualities that lull the conscience of the sinner blind the eyes of the onlookers. People are sentimental, and bastinado wrong-doing not according to its harmfulness, but according to the infamy that has come to attach to it. Undiscerning, they chastise with scorpions the old authentic sins, but spare the new. They do not see that boodling is treason, that blackmail is piracy, that embezzlement is theft, that speculation is gambling, that tax-dodging is larceny, that railroad discrimination is treachery, that the factory labor of children is slavery, that deleterious adulteration is murder. It has not come home to them that the fraudulent promoter "devours widows' houses," that the monopolist "grinds the faces of the poor," that mercenary editors and spellbinders "put bitter for sweet and sweet for bitter." The cloven hoof hides in patent leather; and to-day, as in Hosea's time, the people "are destroyed for lack of knowledge." The mob lynches the red-handed slayer, when it ought to keep a gallows Haman-high for the venal mine inspector, the seller of infected milk, the maintainer of a fire-trap theatre. The child-beater is forever blasted in reputation, but the exploiter of infant toil, or the concocter of a soothing syrup for the drugging of babies, stands a pillar of society. The petty shoplifter is more abhorred than the stealer of a franchise, and the wife-whipper is outcast long before the man who sends his over-insured ship to founder with its crew.

There is a special cause for the condoning of sins committed in the way of business and without personal malice. Business men, as a rule, insist upon a free hand in their dealings, and, since they are conspicuous and influential in the community, they carry with them a considerable part of the non-business world. The leisured, the non-industrial employees, the bulk of professional men, and many public servants, hold to the unmitigated maxim of *caveat emptor*, and accept the chicane of trade as reasonable and legitimate. In England till

1487 any one who knew how to read might commit murder with impunity by claiming "benefit of clergy." There is something like this in the way we have granted quack and fakir and mine operator and railroad company indulgence to commit manslaughter in the name of business.

On the other hand, the active producers, such as farmers and workingmen, think in terms of livelihood rather than of profit, and tend therefore to consider the social bearings of conduct. Intent on well-being rather than on pecuniary success, they are shocked at the lenient judgment of the commercial world. Although they have hitherto deferred to the traders, the producers are losing faith in business men's standards, and may yet pluck up the courage to validate their own ethics against the individualistic, anti-social ethics of commerce.

Still, even if the mass turns vehement,

it is not certain the lash of its censure can reach the cuticle of the sinner. A differentiated society abounds in closed doors and curtained recesses. The murmurs of the alley do not penetrate to the boulevard. The shrieks from the blazing excursion steamer do not invade the distant yacht of her owners. If the curses of tricked depositors never rise to the circles of "high finance" that keep the conscience of the savings-bank wrecker, why should the popular hiss stay the commercial buccaneer? All turns on the power of the greater public to astringe the flaccid conscience of business men until they become stern judges of one another. If we have really entered upon the era of jangling classes, it is, of course, idle to hope for a truly public sentiment upon such matters. Nevertheless, in the past, antiseptic currents of opinion have mounted from the healthy base to the yellowing top of the social tree, and they may do so again.

While idealists are dipping their brushes into the sunset for colors bright enough to paint the Utopias that might be if society were quite made over, one may be pardoned for dreaming of what would be possible, even on the plane of existing institutions, if only in this highly articulated society of ours every one were required to act in good faith, and to do what he had deliberately led others to expect of him.

II

THE GRADING OF SINNERS

THE GRADING OF SINNERS

AMERICAN government, the London *Times* once said, is "cheap and nasty," meaning thereby that the public organs of our democracy are by no means so aloof and self-sufficing as they are abroad. This is especially true of the law-enforcing apparatus. In England the judiciary is far more exalted and independent than it is with us. It is better manned and paid, more stately, more secure, more disdainful of public clamor. Our law officers, on the other hand, are not socially and politically so distinct from the people. Their individuality is not so completely merged in their function as upholders of the majesty of the law. Keenly sensitive to the state of the public mind, they are losing rather than gaining in independence. We dream that we live under a government of laws; we are actually under a government of men and of newspapers.

In a people uncleft by deep class distinctions every man can as censor take
part in the defense of society against evil-
doers. Each of us emits a faint, compulsive
beam, and since the agencies for focusing these into a fierce, withering ray of
indignation become every day more per-
fect, public opinion as regulator of conduct steadily gains on priest and judge
and sheriff. More and more the law-
enforcing machinery slows down the
moment it ceases to be urged by public
sentiment. The accumulation of " dead "
laws in the statute book proves how slight
is its automatic action. Much of the control once embodied in the organs of the
law is coming to be diffused throughout
the community. Constituted authorities
are settling and crumbling; they threaten
to become as obsolete for defense as have
the stone walls of the mediæval city. In
twenty-two years we have lynched over
thirty-three hundred persons as against

about twenty-six hundred legally executed. Moral vengeance, the lynching of the personality rather than the person, is, however, the characteristic rôle of the public. Cell and noose are still needed for the low-browed, but public condemnation is dreadful to the newer types of delinquent. Courts must still try people, if we do not want them to be tried by newspapers; but there never was a time when formal acquittal rehabilitated a man less than it does to-day.

Public opinion has become so mighty a regulator of conduct, not because it has grown wiser, but because of the greater ease of ascertaining, focusing, and directing it. There is nothing to indicate a gain in intelligence at all answering to its enlargement of authority. Now, as ever, the judgments the average man passes upon the conduct of his fellow are casual, inconsistent, and thoughtless. The public sentiment drawn from such sources is not fit to safeguard the paramount interests of society. Like a stupid, flushed giant at bay, the public heeds the little overt offender more than the big covert offender. It resents a pinprick more than a blow at the heart. It parries a frontal stroke, but ignores a flank attack. The key to such folly is to be found in certain crude notions which lie at the base of its moral judgments and lead astray its instinct of self-preservation.

THE ERROR THAT SINNERS OUGHT TO BE GRADED ACCORDING TO BADNESS OF CHARACTER

This criterion favors the new, spreading, and threatening types of wrong-doing as contrasted with the old, stationary types. Mark how its ratings fly in the face of common sense. The highwayman, with his alternative, " Your money or your life! " does less mischief than the entrenched monopolist who offers the

public the option, " Your money or go
without ; " but he is, no doubt, a more
desperate character. The government clerk
who secretly markets advance crop in-
formation would hardly steal overcoats,
whereas the hall thief is equal to the
whole gamut of larceny. The life insurance presidents who let one another have
the use of policy-holders' funds at a third of
the market rate may still be trusted not
to purloin spoons. The official who sells
a gold-brick concern the opportunity to
use the mails is an accomplice in wholesale robbery ; but for all that he has his
scruples against pocket-picking.

No poisoner would shrink from the
slow poisonings of the adulterator, whereas the latter would probably draw the line
at administering a deadly drug to his unsuspecting customer. Despite the essential
identity of their work, the ravisher is undoubtedly a more brutal type than the
procurer, and the cut-throat is coarser than

the bandit who ditches a train in order to rob it. The embezzler who guts a savings bank, the corrupt labor-leader who wields the strike as a blackmailer's club, is virtually the assassin of scores of infants and aged and invalid; yet he has sensibilities that make him far less dangerous in most situations than the housebreaker or the sandbagger. Equally limited are the men responsible for the needless extinction of lives by the car stove, at the grade crossing, before the fenderless trolley-car, on the over-insured hulk, or in the treacherous, unfireproofed apartment house. These partial villains, with their piebald consciences, lack the stigmata of the true criminal type. In their crania Lombroso would miss the marks of atavism. They are not the prey of wicked impulses, not Nature's criminals. Bone of our bone and flesh of our flesh, they are in their wrong-doing merely the creatures of Crooked Thinking and Opportunity.

The grading of sinners according to badness of character goes on the assumption that the wickedest man is the most dangerous. This would be true if men were abreast in their opportunities to do harm. In that case the blackest villain would be the worst scourge of society. But the fact is that the patent ruffian is confined to the social basement, and enjoys few opportunities. He can assault or molest, to be sure; but he cannot betray. Nobody depends on him, so he cannot commit breach of trust, — that arch sin of our time. He does not hold in his hand the safety or welfare or money of the public. He is the clinker, not the live coal; vermin, not beast of prey. To-day the villain most in need of curbing is the respectable, exemplary, trusted personage who, strategically placed at the focus of a spider-web of fiduciary relations, is able from his office-chair to pick a thousand pockets, poison a thousand sick, pollute a thousand minds, or imperil a thousand lives. It is the great-scale, high-voltage sinner that needs the shackle. To strike harder at the petty pickpocket than at the prominent and unabashed person who in a large, impressive way sells out his constituents, his followers, his depositors, his stockholders, his policy-holders, his subscribers, or his customers, is to "strain at a gnat and swallow a camel."

No paradox is it, but demonstrable fact, that, in a highly articulate society, the gravest harms are inflicted, not by the worst men, but by those with virtues enough to boost them into some coign of vantage. The boss who sells out the town and delivers the poor over to filth, disease, and the powers that prey, owes his chance to his engaging good-fellowship and big-heartedness. Some of the most dazzling careers of fraud have behind them long and reassuring records of probity, which have served to bait the trap of villainy.

Not that these decoy-virtues are counterfeit. They are, in fact, so genuine that often the stalwart sinner perseveres in the virtue that has lifted him into the high place he abuses. The legislator conscientiously returns the boodle when he finds he cannot "deliver the goods." The boss stands by his friends to his own hurt. The lobbying lawyer is faithful to his client. The corrupting corporation-president is loyal to his stockholders. The boughten editor never quite overcomes his craft-instinct to print " all the news there is." In a word, the big and formidable sinners are gray of soul, but not black, so that chastisement according to their *character* rather than according to their *deeds* lets them off far too easily.

THE ERROR THAT SINNERS SHOULD BE
GRADED ACCORDING TO THE HARM
THEY INFLICT UPON PARTICULAR IN-
DIVIDUALS

Primitive-minded people abhor the wrong-doer, not from a sense of danger, but out of sympathy with his victim. This is why our mobs lynch for murder, assault, rape, arson, wife-beating, kidnapping, and grave-robbing, but pass over such impersonal offenses as peculation, adulteration, rebating, ballot-fraud, bribery, and grafting. The public, while less ferocious than the mob, is nearly as sentimental. It needs a victim to harrow up its feelings. Villainy must be staged with blue lights and slow music. The injury that is problematic, or general, or that falls in undefined ways upon unknown persons, is resented feebly, or not at all. The fiend who should rack his victim with torments such as typhoid inflicts would be torn to pieces. The villain who should taint his enemy's cup with fever germs would stretch hemp. But — think of it! — the corrupt boss who, in order to extort fat contracts for his firm, holds up for a year the building of a filtration plant designed to deliver his city from the typhoid scourge, and thereby dooms twelve hundred of his townspeople to sink to the tomb through the flaming abyss of fever, comes off scatheless.

The popular symbol for the criminal is a ravening wolf, but alas, few latter-day crimes can be dramatized with a wolf and a lamb as the cast! Your up-to-date criminal presses the button of a social mechanism, and at the other end of the land or the year innocent lives are snuffed out. The immediate sacrifice of human beings to the devil is extinct. But fifteenth-century Marshal de Retz, with his bloody offerings to Satan, has his modern counterpart in the king whose insatiate greed, transmitted noiselessly through administrative belting and shafting, lops off the right hands of Congolese who fail to bring in their dues of rubber; in the avaricious nobleman who, rather than relinquish his lucrative timber concession on the Yalu, pulled the wires that strewed Manchuria with corpses. Yet, thanks to the space that divides sinner from sinned-against, planetary crimes such as these excite far less horror than do the atrocities of Jack the Ripper or black Sam Hose. The public, being leaden of imagination, is moved only by the concrete. It heeds the crass physical act, but overlooks the subtile iniquities that pulse along those viewless filaments of interrelation that bind us together. At the present moment nothing would add so much to the security of life in this country as stern dealing with the patent-medicine dispensers, the quack doctors, the adulterators, the jerry-builders, the rookery landlords, and the carrying corporations. These, however, escape, because the community squanders the vials of its wrath on the old-style, open-air sinner, who has the nerve to look his victims in the face as he strikes.

The childishness of the unguided public appears very clearly from a certain modern instance. What is it that is doing the most to-day to excite wrath against the rich? Is it the clash of capital and labor, the insensate luxury flaunted by the Emerged Tenth, the uncovering of the muddy sources of certain great fortunes, the exposure of colossal frauds by high "captains of industry," the frequent identification of the "men who do things" with the men who "do" people, the revelation of the part played by "business interests" in the debauching of our local governments? No, it is none of these. It is the injuries pedestrians and other users of the highway have suffered from a few reckless drivers of the automobile!

A dense population lives in peace by aid of a protecting social order. Those who rack and rend this social order do worse than hurt particular individuals; they wound society itself. The men who steal elections, who make merchandise of the law, who make justice a mockery, who pervert good custom, who foil the plain public intent, who pollute the wells of knowledge, who dim ideals for hire, — these are, in sober truth, the chiefest sinners. They are cutting the guy ropes that keep the big tent from collapsing on our heads. They should be the first to feel the rod. To spare them because such sins furnish no writhing victim to stir our indignation is as if a ship's passengers should lynch pilferers, but release miscreants caught boring with augers in the vessel's bottom.

As society grows complex, it can be harmed in more ways. Once there were no wrongs against the whole community save treason and sacrilege, and against these, strong reaction habits early grew up in the public mind. Later, our frontier communities learned to react promptly with a rope on the man who furnished whiskey to the Indians, started a prairie fire, cut a levee, spread smallpox, or turned revenue informer. Now, however, there are scores of ways in which the common weal may take hurt, and every year finds society more vulnerable. Each advance to higher organization runs us into a fresh zone of danger, so there is more than ever need to be quick to detect and foil the new public enemies that present themselves.

THE VAIN IMAGINATION THAT THERE ARE EXCELLENCES WHICH CONSTITUTE A SUFFICIENT SET-OFF TO SIN

The proper grading of sinners is skewed by taking into account their education, breeding, manners, piety, or philanthropy. The primitive tribal assembly takes an all-round view of the culprit, and the sentence it pronounces passes upon his walk and conversation as well as upon his guilt. The court of justice, however, wisely throws out such considerations as irrelevant, and narrows down to the question, "What punishment does this deed deserve?" In no other way can men be made to stand on a level before the law. Now, long ago we attained in theory the equality of all men before God, and the equality of all men before the law; but the equality of all men before the bar of public opinion is still to be achieved. No judge would dare show himself such a respecter of persons as is the public. How often clean linen and church-going are accepted as substitutes for right-doing! What a deodorizer is polite society! Who smells the buzzard under his stolen peacock plumes! Any one can sense turpitude in the dingy "hobo," but a well-groomed Captain Kidd, of correct habits, with a family "reared in the lap of luxury" as a background, is well-nigh irresistible.

There are other ways in which sinners profit by the delusion that the cardinal thing in men is something else than good faith. The heads of religious, philanthropic, and educational work have influence, and hence the adept of the Higher Thimblerig seeks by gifts to the cause and by a feigned interest to gain their valuable favor and thus compound with society for his offense. Too often, in their zeal for the special social good committed to their charge, they rashly sacrifice the greater good, and ply the whitewash brush on public enemies. Nothing can check this creeping paralysis of the higher nerve-centres of society but the heartfelt conviction that no fillip to religion, philanthropy, or education can atone for tampering with the underpinning of social order. What, in sooth, are professors, preachers, charity-workers, and organizers of philanthropy but betrayers, if, wrapped up in their immediate aims, they condone the social transgressions of their patrons? Fair play and trustful coöperation, bedded on truth and honesty, are the very foundations of

social existence, without which the higher
life could not endure; and no college,
church, hospital, or social settlement can
avail to counterpoise crime that weakens
these foundations.

The conclusion of the whole matter is
this: —

Our social organization has developed to
a stage where the old righteousness is not
enough. We need an annual supplement to
the Decalogue. The growth of credit institutions, the spread of fiduciary relations,
the enmeshing of industry in law, the interlacing of government and business, the
multiplication of boards and inspectors, —
beneficent as they all are, they invite to sin.
What gateways they open to greed! What
fresh parasites they let in on us! How idle
in our new situation to intone the old
litanies! The reality of this close-knit life
is not to be *seen* and *touched*; it must be
thought. The sins it opens the door to are to

be discerned by knitting the brows rather than by opening the eyes. It takes imagination to see that bogus medical diploma, lying advertisement, and fake testimonial are death-dealing instruments. It takes imagination to see that savings-bank wrecker, loan shark, and investment swindler, in taking livelihoods take lives. It takes imagination to see that the business of debauching voters, fixing juries, seducing law-makers, and corrupting public servants is like sawing through the props of a crowded grand-stand. Whether we like it or not, we are in the organic phase, and the thickening perils that beset our path can be beheld only by the mind's eye.

The problem of security is therefore being silently transformed. Blind, instinctive reactions are no longer to be trusted. Social defense is coming to be a matter for the expert. The rearing of dikes against faithlessness and fraud calls for intelligent social engineering. If in this strait the public does not speedily become far shrewder in the grading and grilling of sinners, there is nothing for it but to turn over the defense of society to professionals.

III

THE CRIMINALOID

THE CRIMINALOID

THE Edda has it that during Thor's visit to the giants he is challenged to lift a certain gray cat. "Our young men think it nothing but play." Thor puts forth his whole strength, but can at most bend the creature's back and lift one foot. On leaving, however, the mortified hero is told the secret of his failure. "The cat — ah! we were terror-stricken when we saw one paw off the floor; for that is the Midgard serpent which, tail in mouth, girds and keeps up the created world."

How often to-day the prosecutor who tries to lay by the heels some notorious public enemy is baffled by a mysterious resistance! The thews of Justice become as water; her sword turns to lath. Though the machinery of the law is strained askew, the evil-doer remains erect, smiling, unscathed. At the end, the mortified champion of the law may be given to understand that, like Thor, he was contending with the established order; that he had unwittingly laid hold on a pillar of society, and was therefore pitting himself against the reigning organization in local finance and politics.

The real weakness in the moral position of Americans is not their attitude toward the plain criminal, but their attitude toward the quasi-criminal. The shocking leniency of the public in judging conspicuous persons who have thriven by antisocial practices is not due, as many imagine, to sycophancy. Let a prominent man commit some offense in bad odor and the multitude flings its stones with a right good will. The social lynching of the self-made magnate who put away his faded, toil-worn wife for the sake of a soubrette, proves that the props of the old morality have not rotted through. Sex righteousness continues to be thus stiffly upheld simply because man has not been inventing new ways of wronging woman. So long ago were sex sins recognized and branded that the public, feeling sure of itself, lays on with promptness and emphasis. The slowness of this same public in lashing other kinds of transgression betrays, not sycophancy or unthinking admiration of success, but perplexity. The prosperous evil-doers that bask undisturbed in popular favor have been careful to shun — or seem to shun — the familiar types of wickedness. Overlooked in Bible and Prayer-book, their obliquities lack the brimstone smell. Surpass as their misdeeds may in meanness and cruelty, there has not yet been time enough to store up strong emotion about them; and so the sight of them does not let loose the flood of wrath and abhorrence that rushes down upon the long-attainted sins.

The immunity enjoyed by the perpetrator of new sins has brought into being a class for which we may coin the term *criminaloid.*[1] By this we designate such as prosper by flagitious practices which have not yet come under the effective ban of public opinion. Often, indeed, they are guilty in the eyes of the law; but since they are not culpable in the eyes of the public and in their own eyes, their spiritual attitude is not that of the criminal. The lawmaker may make their misdeeds crimes, but, so long as morality stands stock-still in the old tracks, they escape both punishment and ignominy. Unlike their low-browed cousins, they occupy the cabin rather than the steerage of society. Relentless pursuit hems in the criminals, narrows their range of success, denies them influence. The criminaloids, on the other hand, encounter but feeble opposition, and, since their practices are often more lucrative than the authentic crimes, they distance their more scrupulous rivals in

---

[1] Like *asteroid, crystalloid, anthropoid,* etc. "Criminaloid" is Latin-Greek, to be sure, but so is " *sociology.*"

business and politics and reap an uncommon worldly prosperity.

Of greater moment is the fact that the criminaloids lower the tone of the community. The criminal slinks in the shadow, menacing our purses but not our ideals; the criminaloid, however, does not belong to the half world. Fortified by his connections with "legitimate business," "the regular party organization," perhaps with orthodoxy and the *bon ton*, he may even bestride his community like a Colossus. In his sight *and in their own sight* the old-style, square-dealing sort are as grasshoppers. Do we not hail him as "a man who does things," make him director of our banks and railroads, trustee of our hospitals and libraries? When Prince Henry visits us, do we not put him on the reception committee? He has far more initial weight in the community than has the clergyman, editor, or prosecutor who arraigns him. From his example and his excuses spreads an influence that tarnishes the ideals of ingenuous youth on the threshold of active life. To put the soul of this pagan through a Bertillon system and set forth its marks of easy identification is, therefore, a sanitary measure demanded in the interest of public health.

THE KEY TO THE CRIMINALOID IS NOT EVIL IMPULSE BUT MORAL INSENSIBILITY

The director who speculates in the securities of his corporation, the banker who lends his depositors' money to himself under divers corporate aliases, the railroad official who grants a secret rebate for his private graft, the builder who hires walking delegates to harass his rivals with causeless strikes, the labor leader who instigates a strike in order to be paid for calling it off, the publisher who bribes his text-books into the schools, these reveal in their faces nothing of wolf or vulture. Nature has not foredoomed them to evil by a double dose of lust, cruelty, malice, greed, or jealousy.

They are not degenerates tormented by monstrous cravings. They want nothing more than we all want, — money, power, consideration, — in a word, success; but they are in a hurry and they are not particular as to the means.

The criminaloid prefers to prey on the anonymous public. He is touchy about the individual victim, and, if faced down, will even make him reparation out of the plunder gathered at longer range. Too squeamish and too prudent to practice treachery, brutality, and violence himself, he takes care to work through middlemen. Conscious of the antipodal difference between doing wrong and getting it done, he places out his dirty work. With a string of intermediaries between himself and the toughs who slug voters at the polls, or the gang of navvies who break other navvies' heads with shovels on behalf of his electric line, he is able to keep his hands sweet and his boots clean. Thus he becomes a consumer of custom-made crime, a client of criminals, oftener a maker of criminals by persuading or requiring his subordinates to break law. Of course he must have "responsible" agents as valves to check the return flow of guilt from such proceedings. He shows them the goal, provides the money, insists on "results," but vehemently declines to know the foul methods by which alone his understrappers can get these "results." Not to bribe, but to employ and finance the briber; not to lie, but to admit to your editorial columns "paying matter;" not to commit perjury, but to hire men to homestead and make over to you claims they have sworn were entered in good faith and without collusion; not to cheat, but to promise a "rake-off" to a mysterious go-between in case your just assessment is cut down; not to rob on the highway, but to make the carrier pay you a rebate on your rival's shipments; not to shed innocent blood, but to bribe inspectors to overlook your neglect to install safety appliances: such are the ways of the criminaloid. He is a buyer rather than a practitioner of sin, and his middlemen spare him unpleasant details.

Secure in his quilted armor of lawyer-spun sophistries, the criminaloid promulgates an ethics which the public hails as a disinterested contribution to the philosophy of conduct. He invokes a pseudo-Darwinism to sanction the revival of outlawed and by-gone tactics of struggle. Ideals of fellowship and peace are "unscientific." To win the game with the aid of a sleeveful of aces proves one's fitness to survive. A sack of spoil is Nature's patent of nobility. A fortune is a personal attribute, as truly creditable as a straight back or a symmetrical face. Poverty, like the misshapen ear of the degenerate, proves inferiority. The wholesale fleecer of trusting, workaday people is a "Napoleon," a "superman." Labor defending its daily bread must, of course, obey the law; but "business," especially the "big proposition," may free itself of such trammels in the name of a "higher law." The censurers of the criminaloid are "pin-headed disturbers" who would imitate him if they had the chance or the brains.

THE CRIMINALOID IS NOT ANTI-SOCIAL BY NATURE

Nation-wide is the zone of devastation of the adulterator, the rebater, the commercial free-booter, the fraud promoter, the humbug healer, the law-defying monopolist. State-wide is the burnt district of the corrupt legislator, the corporation-owned judge, the venal inspector, the bought bank examiner, the mercenary editor. But draw near the sinner and he whitens. If his fellow men are wronged clear to his doorstep he is criminal, not criminaloid. For the latter loses his sinister look, even takes on a benign aspect, as you come close. Within his home town, his ward, his circle, he is perhaps a good man, if judged by the simple old-time tests. Very likely he keeps his marriage vows, pays his debts, "mixes" well, stands by his friends, and has a contracted kind of public spirit. He is ready enough to rescue imperiled babies, protect maidens, or help poor widows. He is unevenly moral: oak in the family and clan virtues, but basswood in commercial and civic ethics. In some relations he is more sympathetic and generous than his critics; and he resents with genuine feeling the scorn of men who happen to have specialized in other virtues than those that appeal to him. Perhaps his point of honor is to give bribes but not to take them; perhaps it is to "stay bought" or not to sell out to both sides at once.

The type is exemplified by the St. Louis boodler, who, after accepting $25,000 to vote against a certain franchise, was offered a larger sum to vote for it. He did so, but returned the first bribe. He was asked on the witness-stand why he had returned it. "Because it was n't mine!" he exclaimed, flushing with anger. "I had n't earned it."

Seeing that the conventional sins are mostly close-range inflictions, whereas the long-range sins, being recent in type, have not yet been branded, the criminaloid receives from his community the credit of the close-in good he does, but not the shame of the remote evil he works.

Sometimes it is *time* instead of *space* that divides him from his victims. It is to-morrow's morrow that will suffer from the patent soothing-syrup, the factory toil of infants, the grabbing of public lands, the butchery of forests, and the smuggling in of coolies. In such a case the short-sighted many exonerate him; only the far-sighted few mark him for what he is. Or it may be a social interval that leaves him his illusion of innocence. Like Robin Hood, the criminaloid spares his own sort and finds his quarry on another social plane. The labor grafter, the political "striker," and the blackmailing society editor prey upward; the franchise grabber, the fiduciary thief, and the frenzied financier prey downward. In either case the sinner moves in an atmosphere of friendly approval and can still any smart of conscience with the balm of good fellowship and adulation.

It is above all the political criminaloid who is social. We are assured that the king of the St. Louis boodlers is "a good fellow, — by nature, at first, then by profession." "Everywhere big Ed went, there went a smile also and encouragement for your weakness, no matter what it was." The head of the Minneapolis ring was "a good fellow — a genial, generous reprobate," "the best-loved man in the community," "especially good to the poor." "Stars-and-Stripes Sam" was the nickname of a notorious looter of Philadelphia, who amassed influence by making "a practice

of going to lodges, associations, brother-
hoods, Sunday-schools, and all sort of public and private meetings, joining some, but
making at all speeches patriotic and sentimental." The corrupt boss of another
plundered city is reported to be " a charm-
ing character," possessing " goodness of
heart and personal charm," and loved for
his " genial, hearty kindness." He shrank
from robbing anybody; he was equal, however, to robbing everybody. Of this type
was Tweed, who had a "good heart," do-
nated $50,000 to the poor of New York,
and was sincerely loved by his clan.

It is now clear why hot controversy
rages about the unmasked criminaloid. His
home town, political clan, or social class
insists that he is a good man maligned,
that his detractors are purblind or jealous.
The criminaloid is really a borderer between the camps of good and evil, and this
is why he is so interesting. To run him to
earth and brand him, as long ago pirate and

traitor were branded, is the crying need of our time. For this Anak among malefactors, working unchecked in the rich field of sinister opportunities opened up by latter-day conditions, is society's most dangerous foe, more redoubtable by far than the plain criminal, because he sports the livery of virtue and operates on a Titanic scale. Every year that sees him pursue in insolent triumph his nefarious career raises up a host of imitators and hurries society toward moral bankruptcy.

THE CRIMINALOID PRACTICES A PROTECTIVE MIMICRY OF THE GOOD

Because so many good men are pious, the criminaloid covets a high seat in the synagogue as a valuable private asset. Accordingly he is often to be found in the assemblies of the faithful, zealously exhorting and bearing witness. Onward thought he must leave to honest men; his line is strict orthodoxy. The upright may fall slack in devout observances, but he cannot afford to neglect his church connection. He needs it in his business. Such simulation is easier because the godly are slow to drive out the open-handed sinner who eschews the conventional sins. Many deprecate prying into the methods of any brother " having money or goods ostensibly his own or under a title not disapproved by the proper tribunals." They have, indeed, much warrant for insisting that the saving of souls rather than the salvation of society is the true mission of the church.

The old Hebrew prophets, to be sure, were intensely alive to the anti-social aspect of sin. They clamor against " making the ephah small and the shekel great," falsifying the balances, " treading upon the poor." " Sensational," almost "demagogic," is their outcry against those who " turn aside the stranger in his right," " take a bribe," " judge not the cause of the fatherless," " oppress the hireling in his wages," " take

increase," "withhold the pledge," "turn
aside the poor in the gate from their right,"
"take away the righteousness of the righteous from him." No doubt, their stubborn
insistence that God wants "mercy and not
sacrifice," despises feast days, delights not
in burnt offerings, will not hear the melody
of viols, but desires judgment to "run down
as waters, and righteousness as a mighty
stream," struck their contemporaries as ex-
treme. Over against their antiquated outlook may be set the "larger view" that our
concern should be for the sinner rather than
the sinned-against. He is in peril of hell
fire, whereas the latter risks nothing more
serious than loss, misery, and death. After
all, sin's overshadowing effect is the pol-
lution of the sinner's soul; and so it may
be more Christian not to scourge forth the
traffickers from the Temple, but to leave
them undisturbed where good seed may
perchance fall upon their flinty souls.

Likewise the criminaloid counterfeits

the good citizen. He takes care to meet all the conventional tests, — flag worship, old-soldier sentiment, observance of all the national holidays, perfervid patriotism, party regularity and support. Full well he knows that the giving of a fountain or a park, the establishing of a college chair on the Neolithic drama or the elegiac poetry of the Chaldæans, will more than outweigh the dodging of taxes, the grabbing of streets, and the corrupting of city councils. Let him have his way about charters and franchises, and he zealously supports that "good government" which consists in sweeping the streets, holding down the "lid," and keeping taxes low. Nor will he fail in that scrupulous correctness of private and domestic life which confers respectability. In politics, to be sure, it is often necessary to play the "good fellow;" but in business and finance a studious conformity to the *convenances* is of the highest importance. The criminaloid must perforce seem sober and chaste, "a good husband and a kind father." If in this respect he offend, his hour of need will find him without support, and some callow reporter or district attorney will bowl him over like any vulgar criminal.

The criminaloid therefore puts on the whole armor of the good. He stands having his loins girt about with religiosity and having on the breastplate of respectability. His feet are shod with ostentatious philanthropy, his head is encased in the helmet of spread-eagle patriotism. Holding in his left hand the buckler of worldly success and in his right the sword of "influence," he is "able to withstand in the evil day, and having done all, to stand."

THE CRIMINALOID PLAYS THE SUPPORT OF HIS LOCAL OR SPECIAL GROUP AGAINST THE LARGER SOCIETY

The plain criminal can do himself no good by appealing to his "Mollies," "Larrikins," or "Mafiosi," for they have no social standing. The criminaloid, however, identifies himself with some legitimate group, and when arraigned he calls upon his group to protect its own. The politically influential Western land thieves stir up the slumbering local feeling against the "impertinent meddlers" of the forestry service and the land office. Safe behind the judicial dictum that "bribery is merely a conventional crime," the boodlers denounce their indicter as "blackening the fair fame" of his state, and cry "Stand up for the grand old commonwealth of Nemaha!" The city boss harps artfully on the chord of local spirit and summons his bailiwick to rebuke the up-state reformers who would unhorse him. The law-breaking saloon-keeper rallies merchants with the cry that enforcement of the liquor laws "hurts business." The labor grafter represents his exposure as a capitalist plot and calls upon all Truss Riveters to "stand pat" and "vindicate" him with a reëlection.

When a pious buccaneer is brought to bay, the Reverend Simon Magus thus sounds the denominational bugle: "Brother Barabbas is a loyal Newlight and a generous supporter of the Newlight Church. This vicious attack upon him is therefore a covert thrust at the Newlight body and ought to be resented by all the brethren." High finance, springing to the help of self-confessed thieves, meets an avenging public in this wise: "The Integrity Trust not only seeks with diabolical skill a reputation to blast, but, once blasted, it sinks into it wolfish fangs and gloats over the result of its fiendish act;" and adds, "This is not the true American spirit."

Here twangs the ultimate chord! For in criminaloid philosophy it is "un-American" to wrench patronage from the hands of spoilsmen, "un-American" to deal Federal justice to rascals of state eminence, "un-American" to pry into "private arrangements" between shipper and carrier,

" un-American " to fry the truth out of re-
luctant magnates.

The claims of the wider community
have no foe so formidable as the scared
criminaloid. He is the champion of the
tribal order as against the civil order. By
constantly stirring up on his own behalf
some sort of clannishness — local, sec-
tional, partisan, sectarian, or professional
clannishness — he rekindles dying jealousies and checks the rise of the civic spirit.
It is in line with this clannishness that he
wants citizens to act together on a personal
basis. He does not know what it is to
rally around a principle. Fellow partisans
are " friends." To scratch or to bolt is to
" go back on your friends." The criminaloid understands sympathy and antipathy
as springs of conduct, but justice strikes
him as hardly human. The law is a club to
rescue your friends from and to smite your
enemies with, but it has no claim of its own.
He expects his victims to " come back "

at him if they can, but he cannot see why everything may not be "arranged," "settled out of court." Those inflexible prosecutors who hew to the line and cannot be "squared" impress him as fanatical and unearthly, as monsters who find their pleasure in making trouble for others. For to his barbarian eyes society is all a matter of "stand in."

So long as the public conscience is torpid, the criminaloid has no sense of turpitude. In the dusk and the silence the magic of clan opinion converts his misdeeds into something rich and strange. For the clan lexicon tells him that a bribe is a "retaining fee," a railroad pass is a "courtesy," probing is "scandal-mongering," the investigator is an "officious busybody," a protest is a "howl," critics are "foul harpies of slander," public opinion is "unreasoning clamor," regulation is "meddling," any inconvenient law is a "blue" law. As rebate-giver he is sustained by the assurance that "in Rome you must do as the Romans do." As disburser of corruption funds he learns that he is but "asserting the higher law which great enterprises have the right to command." Blessed phrases these! What a lint for dressing wounds to self-respect! Often the reminiscent criminaloid, upon comparing his misdeeds with what his clansmen stood ready to justify him in doing, is fain to exclaim with Lord Clive, "By God, sir, at this moment I stand amazed at my own moderation!" When the revealing flash comes and the storm breaks, his difficulty in getting the public's point of view is really pathetic. Indeed, he may persist to the end in regarding himself as a martyr to "politics," or "yellow journalism," or the "unctuous rectitude" of personal foes, or "class envy" in the guise of a moral wave.

THE CRIMINALOID FLOURISHES UNTIL
THE GROWTH OF MORALITY OVER-
TAKES THE GROWTH OF OPPORTUNITY
TO PREY

It is of little use to bring law abreast of
the time if morality lags. In a swiftly
changing society the law inevitably tarries
behind need, but public opinion tarries behind need even more. Where, as with us,
the statute has little force of its own, the
backwardness of public opinion nullifies
the work of the legislator. Every added
relation among men makes new chances
for the sons of Belial. Wider interdepend-
encies breed new treacheries. Fresh opportunities for illicit gain are continually
appearing, and these are eagerly seized by
the unscrupulous. The years between the
advent of these new sins and the general
recognition of their heinousness are few or
many according to the alertness of the
social mind. By the time they have been

branded, the onward movement of society has created a fresh lot of opportunities, which are, in their turn, exploited with impunity. It is in this gap that the criminaloid disports himself. The narrowing of this gap depends chiefly on the faithfulness of the vedettes that guard the march of humanity. If the editor, writer, educator, clergyman, or public man is zealous to reconnoitre and instant to cry aloud the dangers that present themselves in our tumultuous social advance, a regulative opinion quickly forms and the new sins soon become odious.

Now, it is the concern of the criminaloids to delay this growth of conscience by silencing the alert vedettes. To intimidate the moulders of opinion so as to confine the editor to the "news," the preacher to the "simple Gospel," the public man to the "party issues," the judge to his precedents, the teacher to his text-books, and the writer to the classic themes — such are the tactics of the criminaloids. Let them but have their way, and the prophet's message, the sage's lesson, the scholar's quest, and the poet's dream would be sacrificed to the God of Things as They Were.

IV

THE GRILLING OF SINNERS

THE GRILLING OF SINNERS

THE American people finds itself to-day in the position of a man with dulled knife and broken cudgel in the midst of an ever-growing circle of wolves. The old regulative system is falling to pieces. Few of the strong and ambitious have any longer the fear of God before their eyes. Hell is looked upon as a bogy for children. The Gospel ideals are thought unscientific. As for the courts, they seem to have nothing but blank cartridges for the bigger beasts of prey. Upon the practicers of new sins there is no longer a curb unless it be public censure. So the question of the hour is, Can there be fashioned out of popular senti-ment some sort of buckler for society? Can our loathing of rascals be wrought up into a kind of unembodied government, able to restrain the men that derisively snap their fingers at the agents of the law?

That the public scorn really bites into
wrong-doers of the modern type may be
read in the fate of the insurance gang.
If, as some assert, American society were
already split into classes, each with its
standards and its opinions, these robbers
would have taken asylum with their own
class, and from the thick of their " crowd "
would have waved a gay and mocking
hand at the wrathful public. Haughty Ro-
man patricians, Spanish *hidalgos*, French
seigneurs, or British noblemen would have
done so, heeding the curses of the com-
monalty no more than the chattering of
daws. But the insurance thieves were
self-made Americans, country-bred, genial,
sensitive, uncarapaced by pride of caste.
Their sense of superiority was, after all,
a short and feeble stalk that soon wilted.
They *did* care what people thought of
them, and so to the grave or to exile they
fled from the vitriol spray of censure. If
only we can bring it to bear, the respect

or scorn of the many is still an immense asset of society in its struggle with sinners.

The community need feel no qualm when lashing the sinner. We are bidden to forgive our enemies, but not the enemies of our society, our posterity. For society to "resist not evil" would be folly, because for most of us society's attitude fixes the guiding ideas of right and wrong. Any outrage we can practice with impunity comes finally to be looked upon as a matter of course. To the aggressor the non-resisting community practically says, "Trample me, please. Thanks!" Thus it becomes a partner in his misdeeds. The public that turns the other cheek tempts a man to fresh sinning. It makes itself an accomplice in the undoing of a soul. It is the indulgent parent spoiling the child. It is therefore our sacred duty, not lazily to condone, but vigorously to pursue and castigate the sinner. It is sad but true that the community is prompter to correct the wife-beater than the rebater or the dummy director. Such indifference to the soul's health of eminent citizens is deplorable.

There is fair hope that out of public opinion a means of rational defense may be developed, provided only we renounce certain false notions which now hinder the proper grilling of sinners.

THE FALLACY THAT SINNERS SHOULD BE CHASTISED ONLY BY THEIR BETTERS

Sometimes the hounded sinner reminds us through his spokesman that "He moves in a higher world into which we may not enter." Oftener he counters by saying, — if his sinning is *very* lucrative it will be said for him, — "In my place, you, too, would have bribed the inspector, or doctored the goods, or exacted the rebate." "He that is without sin among you, let him first cast a stone." In this vein an apologist sneers, "Those who are chattering about predatory wealth would not refuse to take over corporation stock even in the R—— properties." The truth is, however, the censor need not take the attitude of "I am holier than thou." What if the critics are no better than they should be? Sinners are scourged, not to proclaim their moral inferiority, but to brace people to resist temptation. May not a weak man, untempted, prop a stronger man who is under temptation? Opportunity puts one's baser self in the saddle; whereas the comment of the disinterested spectator utters his better self. If the baser self of the tempted man could not profit by the rebuke of a public made up of men no better than he is, many of us would fall into the ditch.

Slow, indeed, would be moral uplift, if the public allowed itself to be silenced by the *tu quoque* of the malefactor. Of course it would be inspiring to be charmed on

from height to height by the voices of seers
and the example of heroes. But Isaiahs
and Savonarolas are rare; and certain practices must be outlawed at once if we are
not to rot down together. In meeting new
forms of sin, we have nothing to rely on
but the common conscience ; that is, the
deliverance of the best selves of most of us.
It is the neutrals, not the belligerents, that
humanize warfare. It is the onlookers, not
the champions, that uphold the rules of
the ring. Not because they are better men,
but because they are in a less trying position. So it will be not the quickened consciences of the principals, but the hisses
of the crowd on the bleachers, that will
protect shipper from railroad, lift the
plane of business competition, restrain
the oppression of workingmen, and stop
the feeding of human seed-corn to swine.

THE ERROR THAT SOCIETY'S CASTIGATION
OF THE SINNER IS MERELY THE ASSER-
TION OF THE SELF-INTEREST OF THE
MANY

Back Bay stockholders are assured that
Iowa's maximum rate law is a shameless
cheapening of railroad services by the
banded customers of the road, and ought
to be defied. Gas magnates snap their fingers
at municipal regulations on the pretext that
such ordinances express only the self-interest of gas consumers. Employers flout factory laws on the ground that the legislature
stood in awe of " the labor vote." In some
circles the feeling is growing up that obedience is the part of a dastard. The money-
maker begins to insist that the inconvenient
law embodies nothing but the will of the
stronger or bigger class bent on oppressing
the weaker or fewer, and claims the right
to break such a law if he can. Now, this
is moral gangrene, so deadly that no one

with the infection ought to have place or influence in society.

The truth is, law is shot through and through with conscience. The uprising against rebating, or monopoly, or fiduciary sin, registers, not the self-interest of the many, but the general sense of right. To be sure, an agitation against company stores, or the two-faced practices of directors, may start as the "We won't stand it" of a victimized class; but when it solicits general support it takes the form "These things are wrong," and it can triumph only when it chimes with the common conscience. In the case of child labor, night work for women, crimping and peonage, the opposition springs up among onlookers rather than among victims, and is chivalric from the beginning. The fact is, the driving force of the great sunward movement now on is moral indignation. Not one of the attempts to shackle the newer stripe of depredators lends itself to interpretation in terms of self-interest. In every instance the slogan has been, not " Protect yourselves," but " Put down iniquity ! "

The special-interest man ignores the moral energy that inspires the uprising against latter-day sin. He scoffs at a law on the ground that it was enacted by a bare majority of " hayseed " legislators, ignorant of legal philosophy and the fitness of things. He does not care to notice that this close vote records an overwhelming public sentiment, the outcome of a long, disinterested agitation. Or he complains that the statute is " precipitate," and pleads for "conservatism."

" Conservatism ! " piled on top of inertia and the strangle-hold of sinister interests, in a tumultuously changing society, where an evil condition may be rapidly worsening while we speechify and procrastinate! Here is a growing evil, — so much blood of brakemen on cars and rails. Give heed, ye legislators ! No impression. The legislator removes his cigar long enough to sneer, "hot air," "mawkish sentimentality," "they take the risks." So, on with the slaughter! Let the wheels redden until the totals are formidable. "Now will you act?" No, "interference" would "undermine individual responsibility," or be "unconstitutional." So let the mangled pile up, until, like the cuirassiers in the ravine at Waterloo, their bodies fill to the brink the chasm of selfish incredulity. So is it with the uprooting of child labor. Once the pocket-book interest has twined itself about the evil, the wreckage of child life has to be mountainous, ghastly, and sickening, before the public can be stirred to the point of breaking the grasp of the employers on the throat of the legislature. The same obstacles delay the advent of mine inspection, tenement-house reform, the abolition of grade crossings, the enforced fencing of dangerous machinery. Thanks to the inertia of large bodies and the power of special interests, the relief inevitably comes ten to twenty years later than it should. To add, now, conscious " conservatism," is like setting the brake on an overloaded wagon being hauled up the bare western slope of a sandy hill on a July afternoon!

THE DELUSION THAT THE NONCONFORM-IST IS THE REAL PERIL TO SOCIETY

It is human nature to resent difference, and the time was when people could afford to go asunder on the width of a hat brim or the form of baptism. But such stress on the non-essential is sheer folly, now that the times summon us to close ranks and war down the Newer Unrighteousness.

Public opinion as lord of conduct is not old, — less than a century, in fact. It could not arrive until the weakening of caste, class, and local barriers allowed the "public" to form. Even to-day, the American public is too incoherent to make a good policeman.

Besides the antipathy between whites and blacks, there is the friction between natives and immigrants, the feeling between Christians and Jews, Protestants and Catholics, the inter-denominational jealousies, the mistrust of the churchless, the gulf between Philistia and Bohemia, the chasm between alley and avenue. Although its class barriers are lower, American society is more deeply cleft by race and nationality than is western Europe. Inter-confessional friction is greater here than in the all-Catholic or all-Protestant societies. Thus it is that in seeking to focus the indignation of the law-abiding, we are hampered by a lot of hold-over antipathies. "First things first." To-day the distinction between righteous and sinners is *the main thing*, for upon a lively consciousness of that distinction rests the hope of transmitting our institutions undecayed, of preserving our democratic ideals, of avoiding stratification and class rancor. Yet most people act as if something else were the main thing. They see conduct in the false perspective of a Chinese drawing, where a glance tells you that the man approaching in the middle distance will surely overtop the house in the foreground! Just as in the South the senseless agitation of the race question is delivering that section into the hands of the railroad corporations; just as in the Far West Mormonism is a red herring to drag across the trail of some iniquity when the public is hot on the scent; just as " Catholicism in the schools" raises a dust behind which franchise grabbers can operate; so the divisions and cross-purposes of decent people give the sinner his chance to get away.

It is the honest man who falls into heresy. But the latter-day sinner is sleek, orthodox, and unoffending. He conforms in everything save conduct. No one can outdo him in lip homage to the law and the prophets. It is the law-abiding who are scandalized by one another's nonconformity. They split on beliefs and practices because they care for such things. But men who take the cash register for their compass are nobly tolerant. This is why, in these times that try men's fortunes, sinners rush to one another's aid, excuse and support one another under fire. The monopolists, small and great, local and national, grope their way to one another, strike hands, and as " captains of industry " present to their critics an unbroken front. The security jugglers, from the county-seat town to Wall Street, feel that as " authors of prosperity " an injury to one is the concern of all. Adulterators and commercial crooks rally as " enterprising business men." The puppets of the Interests, from the town council to Congress, stand together as " statesmen." On the other hand, the public they plunder, like Martha " troubled about many things," divides on race, creed, or style, pelts the nonconformist more than the sinner, and lays on a little finger where

it ought to wield a fist. Thus the wolves
hunt in packs, while the watchdogs snap
at one another!

At a moment when the supremacy of
law trembles in the balance, when our leading railroad magnate complains that it is
not easy to carry on a railroad business, "if
you always have to turn to the legal department and find whether you may or may
not," how bootless seem agitations to put
"God" into the Constitution, to enforce
strict Sabbath observance, to break up secret
societies, or to banish negroes to the Jim
Crow car! These fatuous crusades against
Gorky and Madame Andrieva, against
"Mrs. Warren's Profession," against "an-
archist" immigrants, against the Mor-
mons, against undraped statuary, or the
"un-American" labor union, or the for-
eigner's Sunday beer, recall to mind the
monks of Constantinople, wrangling over
the nature of the Trinity while the Turks
were forcing the gates!

In a national war, the common peril hushes petty discords and attunes differing men to harmonious efforts. *But to-day is war-time*. Our assailants are none the less formidable because they grew up among us and walk the same streets. While the wizards of smokeless powder and submarine boat have been making us secure against alien foes, we have grown into an organic society in which the welfare of all is at the mercy of each. The supreme task of the hour is to get together and build a rampart of moral standard, statute, inspection, and publicity, to check the onslaught of internal enemies.

THE FALSE DOCTRINE THAT THE REPRESSION OF THE VICIOUS IS MORE IMPORTANT THAN THE REPRESSION OF SINNERS

By *vice* we mean practices that harm one's self; by *sin* we mean conduct that harms another. They spring from different roots and call for different treatment. Sin grows largely out of the relations into

which men enter, and hence social development, by constantly opening new doors to
wrong-doing, calls into being new species
of sin. Rude law recognizes three kinds of
stealing, developed law ten kinds, the law of
to-day seventeen kinds. By the time it is
abreast of our present needs, it will discrim-
inate perhaps thirty kinds. The same is true
of other types of wrong-doing. Vice, on the
other hand, being personal, is less affected
by social change. New forms, like the
cocaine habit or bridge gambling, are *in-
vented*, not developed by social growth.

As a disease of the social body, vice differs
as much from sin as scrofula from *locomotor
ataxia*. Vice encounters barriers fixed by
nature; in the end its wage is death. Sin,
on the other hand, flourishes if society does
not make haste to check it. The unopposed
sinner makes his way upward towards sunshine, whereas the unchecked vicious man
gravitates toward night. The spectacle of
vice, sleek, honored, and envied, is not pos-

sible, for a practice that works out this way is not vice. But the sight of the unpunished and unrepentant sinner, successful and honored, shocks the righteous, disheartens the weak, and demoralizes the young, who ought to cherish, for a few years at least, the ennobling illusion that the right always triumphs.

Like a ship with a foul bottom, a nation heavily weighted with lewd, drunken, and gaming members cannot keep up with its rivals, and hence the warfare against vice must go on. But efforts should be centred on the young, training and fortifying them to resist the lure of the perilous paths. It is for them we banish or regulate the vice shops, bar obscene literature, and watch the stage. Not so with adults. The effort we expend on persons who go astray with their eyes open is mostly wasted. Usually they cannot be saved, nor are they worth saving. Certainly let vice be made odious. But when the public exerts itself to stamp out drinking and the social evil, it slackens its war on sin, and, moreover, it simply forestalls natural process. Nature limits at last the spread of vice, and the sooner those of congenitally weak will and base impulses eliminate themselves, the better for the race. The go-cart for children by all means, but for adults the stern command, "Stand alone, or if thou canst not stand alone, then fall!" With respect to hell, there is something to be said for the open door. Self-interest, too, is quietly crowding the vicious to the wall. In the end the hard drinkers will be barred from all desirable employments.

Sin, on the contrary, is not self-limiting. If a ring is to be put in the snout of the greedy strong, only organized society can do it. In every new helpful relation the germ of sin lurks, and will create there a pus centre if social antisepsis be lacking. Then how tragic a figure is the victim of sin! To perish of diseased meat to make a packer's dividend is sadder than to perish through one's own thirst for whiskey. The invalid bled by the medical fakirs is more to be pitied than the "sucker" fleeced in the pool-room. For the man who is the prey of the evil inclinations of others surely has a better claim on us than the man who is the prey of his own evil inclinations.

Men rather than women are the natural foes of wrong. Men burn at the spectacle of injustice, women at the sight of suffering. "White," "decent," "fair play," "square deal," voice masculine conscience. Men feel instinctively that the pith of society is orderly struggle, competition tempered by rules of forbearance. The impulse of simple-minded men to put down "foul play" and "dirty work" is a precious safeguard of social order. But the impulses of simple-minded women are not so trustworthy. When they smother red-handed bandits with flowers they are anti-social; when they launch into random vice crusades they

are often little better than pseudo-social.
Now, the rise of great organizations for
focusing the sentiments of millions of
women has lately brought about a certain
effemination of opinion. In the main, this
has been salutary, for it has redressed many
wrongs against women and children, and
exalted the " home " point of view. Yet it
has taught us to hail as "a great moral
triumph " the spectacle of a corporation-
owned legislature obsequiously aiming the
terrors of the law at the grown man who
gives another man a cigarette paper! In the
end, values are so topsy-turvied that a
branch of a famous women's organization
deems it fitting to ask the President of the
United States, " Did you receive sixty bottles of beer from the Brewers' Association,
and did you or your representatives send
the brewers a letter of thanks on White
House stationery for the same package, and
what became of the sixty bottles of beer ?"
The loss of moral leadership by the

clergy is often deplored; but what else is to
be expected, when so many clergymen appeal to the feminine rather than to the masculine conscience? To-day the virile, who
see in graft and monopoly and foul politics
worse enemies than beer, Sunday baseball,
and the army canteen, scoff when the pastor
of the indicted boss of San Francisco pleads,
"He never was known to smoke or take
a drink. He never was seen in front of a
saloon bar." In political battles, the sinister
interests easily rally the religious people by
standing for a "lid on" policy. This throw-
ing over of the vice interests by the corporation interests is the secret of the "good
government" that is the boast of latter-day
commercial oligarchy. In the struggle of a
city to free itself from corporation bond-
age, is not the psychologic moment always
punctuated by a hectoring deputation of
clergymen to summon Mr. Mayor to enforce to the letter the Sunday closing ordinance, followed by a blast from the pulpits

when the mayor declines to play the traction company's little game? Not long ago a reform mayor was discredited because, emerging late from his office, he descended into a basement lunch room, and ate at the same counter with street-walkers and night-birds. The pastors of the strait-laced magnates who had never stooped to anything worse than stealing a street were scandalized at the mayor's elbow-touch with disreputables, and appealed with success to the ossified Puritanism of their flock.

Our moral pace-setters strike at bad personal habits, but act as if there was something sacred about money-making; and, *seeing that the master iniquities of our time are connected with money-making*, they do not get into the big fight at all. The child-drivers, monopoly-builders, and crooked financiers have no fear of men whose thought is run in the moulds of their grandfathers. Go to the tainted-money colleges, and you will learn that Drink, not Graft, is the nation's bane. Visit the religious societies for young men, and you will find personal correctness exalted above the social welfare.

The standards the old Puritans battled for are now established. Organized opposition to them has ceased, and the tide of battle has rolled away to a new quarter. Satan's main onset to-day is on the side of sin, rather than on the side of vice. Therefore the strategy of the situation summons society to draft off more of its forces to the aid of the "social Puritans." Are the accredited leaders of moral sentiment good generals in so heavily shelling the trenches of vice? Are they not slow in recognizing the key positions in the Holy War of to-day?

Let him who doubts where the battle rages mark how fares the assailant of sin. To-day there is little risk in letting fly at the red light. What an easy mark is the "tenderloin"! Rare is the clergyman, teacher, or editor who can be unseated by banded saloon-keepers, gamblers, and madames. Their every "knock" is a boost. If you want a David-and-Goliath fight, you must attack the powers that prey, not on the vices of the lax, but on the necessities of the decent. The deferred-dividend graft, the "yellow dog" fund, the private-car iniquity, the Higher Thimblerig, far from turning tail and slinking away beaten like the vice-caterers, confront us rampant, fire-belching, sabre-toothed, and razor-clawed. They are able to gag critics, hobble investigators, hood the press, and muzzle the law. Drunk with power, in office and club, in church and school, in legislature and court, they boldly make their stand, ruining the innocent, shredding the reputations of the righteous, destroying the careers and opportunities of their assailants, dragging down pastor and scholar, publicist and business man, from livelihood and influence, unhorsing alike faithful public servant, civic champion, and knight-errant of conscience, and all the while gathering into loathsome captivity the souls of multitudes of young men. Here is a fight where blows are rained, and armor dinted, and wounds suffered, and laurels won. If a sworn champion of the right will prove he is a man and not a dummy, let him go up against these!

Because society develops, comes into new situations, runs into strange perils, finds old foes with new faces and enemies masquerading as friends, it is folly to train its guns ever on the same spot. Yesterday's battle-cries of conscience cannot thrill us, and so the battle-cries of to-day may have little meaning for our children's children. They, perhaps, will be worrying about the marriage of the tainted, or the two-child system. Every age has to reconnoitre its foes and mark where they are massing. Like a rudderless steamer on a river of savage Africa, society, caught in the current of evolution, dips, lurches, drifts, swings, exposing now port, now starboard, to the missiles of fresh enemies that present themselves in strange guise at every turn of the stream.

V

SINNING BY SYNDICATE

SINNING BY SYNDICATE

THOSE who contend that men are growing better, and those who insist that matters are growing worse, may both be right. "Look at the amelioration in the lot of women, of children, of blacks, of convicts, of defectives," flute the apologists. "Never were punishments more humane, manners milder, amusements cleaner, gifts larger, the rights of the weak better protected, the lower creatures more considered." "But mark the ruthlessness of industry, the ferocity of business, the friction of classes, the stench of politics," rasp the critics. "Never in our time were children so exploited, workers so driven, consumers so poisoned, passengers so mangled, investors so fleeced, public servants so tempted." The key to the paradox is that while men are improving in their personal relations, the control of industry and business is becoming impersonal.

Take the face-to-face element out of a relation, and any lurking devil in it comes to the surface. In the old South there was a world of difference to the slaves between the kind master and the hard master. But these differences tended to disappear as the plantations grew big and the slaves came under the immediate control of overseers. The Irish found tenancy tolerable under a good landlord; but with absenteeism and the management of the estate by the agent, all that was oppressive in landlordism came out. It is noteworthy that the strife between employer and employee was never so bitter as it has become since corporations came to be the great employers. So, also, the tension between the railroads and the people has grown with the merging of lines locally owned into huge systems controlled by remote investors in the East or in Europe.

There is nothing like distance to disin-fect dividends. Therefore the moral char-acter of the stockholders makes very little difference in the conduct of the affairs of the corporation. Christian or heathen, na-tive or alien, blue blood or plebeian, rich or poor, they all sanction much the same thing, and that is, the policy that promises the biggest dividends in the long run. To the directors their virtual mandate is, "Get results!" The directors pass this mandate to the officers. The officers pass it along to the heads of departments, and these send it on down the line. Take one gas com-pany formed by saints and another formed by sinners. The directors of the two com-panies will be more alike than the stock-holders, the officers will be still more alike, and the men who come into contact with the legislature or the city council, or the gas consumers, will not differ by a shade. The saintly stockholders not only do not know what is going on, but so long as the dividends are comfortable they resent having inconvenient knowledge thrust upon them.

The corporation, to be sure, has certain good points. The corporate owner — of course we are not speaking of one-man corporations, or of those whose officers follow their own sweet will — is not warped by race antipathy or religious prejudice or caste pride. Unlike the individual business man, its course is never shaped by political ambitions or social aspirations or the personal feuds of its wife. It does not exact personal subservience, does not indulge itself in petty tyranny, is not held back from negotiation with its employees by aristocratic haughtiness. It does not feel anger or hold a grudge. If it ruins any one, it does so not from malice, but simply because he stands in the way. Let him meekly creep into the ditch, and it honks by unnoticing. The business man may be swerved by vindictiveness or by generosity, by passion or by conscience, but the genuine corporation responds to but one motive. Toward gain it gravitates with the ruthlessness of a lava stream.

Nevertheless, if the corporate owner is free from the weaknesses of the individual, it escapes also his wholesome limitations. It feels not the restraints that conscience and public sentiment lay on the business man. It fears the law no more, and public indignation far less, than does the individual. You can hiss the bad man, egg him, lampoon him, caricature him, ostracize him and his. Not so with the bad corporation. The corporation, moreover, is not in dread of hell fire. You cannot Christianize it. You may convert its stockholders, animate them with patriotism or public spirit or love of social service; but this will have little or no effect on the tenor of their corporation. In short, it is an entity that transmits the greed of investors, but not their conscience;

that returns them profits, but not unpopularity.

In view of the psychology of the corporation, the fact that in a lifetime it has risen to the captaincy of more than half the active wealth of this country cannot be without a bearing on our moral situation. A current manual describes 6700 companies (not including banking and insurance companies) with a capitalization of thirty-six billions of dollars, and an actual property estimated to be worth twenty-seven billions or sixty per cent of all the wealth of the United States outside of farm values and of city values in residences and in private businesses. Surely the misconduct of this giant race of artificial persons deserves consideration by itself.

MORE THAN OTHER SINNING, CORPORATE SINNING ALIENATES SOCIAL CLASSES

Thanks to the magic of limited liability, every year finds a greater distance between the corporate business and its absentee owners. Every year sees these owners more numerous, more scattered, more dominated by the big insiders. Every year sees savings banks, trust companies, and insurance companies coming between the corporate management and the millions who furnish the money, thereby making it harder for their conscience to reach and humanize that management. Moreover, the Big Men's practice of watering a paying stock and unloading the infusion upon the investing public is marvelously potent in banishing humanity and decency from the corporation's treatment of its labor, its patrons, or the public authorities. To doubt if stockwatering tightens the squeeze is to doubt if the *bona fide* investor, restless on the bare bench of a paltry three per cent per annum, will yammer harder for more dividends than one lounging luxuriously on the velvet of twelve per cent. The device of capitalizing and marketing the last turn of the corporation screw has a diabolic power to convert the retired preacher or professor (who has exchanged his life's savings for aqueous securities at par) into an oppressor of Tennessee miners, or Georgia operatives, or Kansas farmers, as relentless as an absentee Highland laird or a spendthrift Russian nobleman.

These developments tend to bring to the headship of certain big businesses — especially public-service enterprises — men akin to the steward on a feudal estate or the agent of an Irish landlord. With growing remoteness and anonymity of ownership, the railroad, gas, or traction manager who aims to develop his properties, to prosper through the prosperity of the community instead of at its expense, to respect local sentiment, the rights of others, and the law of the land, is dropped. Quietly, but relentlessly, the popular man of local antecedents and attachments, who calls his men "Bill" or "Jim," is discarded for the imported man with "nerve," who "does things," who "gets results" — no matter how. The owners fête and cheer the "efficient" railroad president who has increased the net earnings "520 per cent in eight years," heedless that he lets the trestles rot till cars full of sleeping passengers drop through them, overworks his men till people are hurled to destruction in daily smash-ups, and denies sidings for the swelling traffic till his trainmen pay Death a heavier toll than soldiers in the field.

Now, the stockholders for whom all these iniquitous things are done do not consciously stand for them. They do not will that children should be worn out, workmen maimed, consumers defrauded, the ballot polluted, or public men debauched. They seem to demand such conduct only because they fail to realize what they are doing when they exact the utmost penny. However harmless their intentions, their clamor for fat dividends inevitably throws the management of quasi-public — and some other — businesses into the hands of the domineering-arrogant or the suave-unscrupulous type. The manager represents just one side of the shareholders, namely, their avarice. In other respects he is no more typical of them than the company doctor is typical of physicians or the corporation attorney is typical of lawyers.

The million or million and a half owners of corporation stock in this country are not as a rule law-despising, unpatriotic, or hard-hearted. They are inoffensive American citizens who probably love their country and their fellow men as much as the brakemen or miners or farmers under the corporation harrow. But their amiable traits are not likely to reflect themselves in the officers and managers of their properties. What, then, is more natural than that those in contact with these agents should take them as representative, should estimate the owners by them, and should accordingly foresee an irrepressible conflict between a lawless, anti-social capitalist class and the masses? Thus springs up the delusion of progress by class war, and the mischievous policy of appealing solely to the class interests of workers instead of chiefly to that sense of right and justice which is found at every level and in every quarter of society, and which is the only power that can settle things so that they stay settled. For you cannot sharpen class consciousness without whetting class hatred and loosening social bonds. The only hatred that is wholesome and social and propulsive is the hatred of the righteous for the willfully unrighteous. A reform that follows this line does not breed a reaction.

Aggressive corporation men put in a wrong light not only capitalists, but their opponents as well. In excusing the troubles their arrogance provokes, they pass along to owners biased versions which, by misrepresenting the claims of patrons and laborers, root capitalists generally in the notion that the masses are uppish and heady, and inspire in them a "last ditch" sentiment as foolish as it is dangerous.

Now, the corporation cannot mend itself. More and more it is impersonal and non-moral. More and more the far-away manager is rated as a profit conveyer, and the conduit with the bigger flow is always preferred. It has become a machine, and Mammon is its master. Reform, therefore, will not come from the inside. Those who supply the capital cannot mould it to their better will. But they can change its spirit if they will join with their fellow citizens in restraining the corporation by public opinion and by statute. If the reaction of organized society upon the Gradgrind type of manager is so severe that he

cannot make so much money for his stockholders as a more reasonable and representative type, he will give way to the
better man, and one cause of the needless
alienation of classes will be removed.

IN RESENTING CORPORATE SINS WE MUST
FOLLOW THE MAXIM, " BLAME NOT THE
TOOL, BUT THE HAND THAT MOVES THE
TOOL "

The savage beats the stone he has stum-
bled over without inquiring who left the
stone in his way. Early law punishes brutes
for the harm they do, and the domestic
animal that hurts a human being is *deodand*.
Law now looks farther back, but the public in its short-sightedness is like a stricken
animal biting at the arrow in its flank
instead of charging on the hunter.

In view of the pressure they are under,
what folly to mob the spade men who set
telephone poles where they have no right
to be, rather than the manager in a down-

town office who gives these men their orders! Why execrate the dozing operator or the forgetful engineer, rather than the superiors who exact the long hours that incapacitate for duty? Why lynch the motorman for running over the baby, when he is on a schedule that obliges him to violate the municipal speed ordinance or lose his job? When powder firms or armor-plate companies are caught giving aid to the enemies of their country by furnishing bad plates or poor powder, what childishness to be satisfied when the employees who plugged the blow-holes or "switched the samples" are dismissed with a great show of virtuous indignation, while the instigators go unpunished!

There is no work so dirty or dangerous but that it will attract volunteers pleading wife and babes to support. An economic constraint, more or less harsh, binds the ordinary underlings of a corporation and obliges us, in quest of the one to blame or

punish, to turn to "the men higher up."
Nor is it easy to find the right place to
stop. Whom shall we blame when orders
for automatic signals put in by superintendents of railroads on which heart-rend-
ing collisions have occurred, have been
turned down by the Wall Street owners?
The company claim-adjuster who, by playing on the ignorance, fears, and necessities
of the injured, "bluffs" them out of their
lawful indemnity, insists with truth that,
if he did not cheat the victims, another
man with fewer qualms would be given his
place. The attorney who fights all claims,
just as well as unjust, to the court of last
resort in order to intimidate claimants,
pleads that his corporation will wear them
out anyway, and he might as well hold the
job as some one else.

Ought we, indeed, to flay the legislator
who, under pain of losing the renomina-
tion, votes as he is told on corporation
matters, or the bureau chief who winks

at crooked land entries because he feels at the back of his neck the chill of the axe? He is no hero, to be sure, who eats dirt in order to keep his berth; but if he refuses he will become a martyr, and it is doubtful if we have the right to require martyrdom of anybody. The society that allows its enemies to run the party conventions, or lets unclean hands wield the official axe, has only itself to blame for what follows.

In all such cases the blame meted out should correspond to the degree of actual — not formal — freedom enjoyed by the agent. Society may call upon a man to renounce his champagne and truffles for the right's sake sooner than his cake and jam; to quarrel with his cake and jam sooner than with his bread and butter; to sacrifice his own bread and butter sooner than the bread and butter of his children. In general, as we ascend from the track-layers who grab a street over night to the foreman of the gang, to the superintendent, to the general manager, accountability broadens and the tale of stripes should increase. Still, even the man high up may act under duress. For example, in a certain city a cotton mill wanted a new street opened and larger water mains laid. The city council tabled the request, but an inquiry showed that $15,000 would "fix" the council. The manager, who "did n't believe in doing business that way," held out for over a year. Meantime the mill suffered financially. The directors became restive, investigated, and found that a manager with a Scotch conscience was standing between them and their profits. They dismissed him for a more "practical" man.

In the corporation the men who give orders, but do not take them, are the directors. They enjoy economic freedom. If their scruples cost them a reëlection, their livelihood is not jeopardized. In the will of these men lies the fountain-head of righteousness or iniquity in the policies of the corporation. Here is the moral laboratory where the lust of an additional quarter of a per cent of dividend, on the part of men already comfortable in goods, is mysteriously transmuted into deeds of wrong and lawlessness by remote, obscure employees in terror of losing their livelihood.

THE ANONYMITY OF THE CORPORATION CAN BE MET ONLY BY FIXING ON DIRECTORS THE RESPONSIBILITY FOR CORPORATE SINNING

In enforcing the rules of the game the chief problem is how to restrain corporations. The threat to withdraw the charter alarms no one, for corporations know they are here to stay. Fine the law-breaking officers, and the board of directors by indemnifying them encourages them to do it again. Fine the corporation, and, if its sinning is lucrative, it heeds the fine no more than a flea-bite. Never will the brake of the law grip these slippery wheels until prison doors yawn for the convicted officers of lawless corporations. Even then you cannot fasten upon the officers legal responsibility for much of the iniquity they instigate. For example, to deceive the state insurance commissioners the president of a culpable insurance company directs the actuary to make up a report of such and such a character. He hands it to the treasurer and the auditor who, as required by law, swear that " to the best of their knowledge and belief " it is true. The high officials who screen their mismanagement with this false report have not been obliged to perjure themselves by swearing to it. The law has no hold upon them.

Again, a rich corporation desires legislation favorable to its own interests. The president engages an eminent attorney to draft a bill to that effect. He then takes it to a great law firm versed in practice of a legislative character. "I want you gentlemen to use all proper and legitimate means to secure the passage of this measure. Send the bill to me." The firm gets the measure introduced and then engages the service of a great lobbyist. The lobbyist seeks to influence men who are under obligations to him for financial aid in getting elected. If some needed legislators stand out demanding money, he engages the services of small lobbyists, or sends an intermediary with a bribe. Thus the chief offenders protect themselves by working through accomplices, in many cases so remote from them that they are not even aware of the accomplices' existence.

Until the courts recast their definitions of legal evidence and legal responsibility, much of the control of corporations must devolve upon some agent free from the pedantries and Byzantism of the law. Public opinion, however, is impotent so long as it allows itself to be kept guessing which shell the pea is under, whether the accountability is with the foreman, or the local manager, or the general manager, or the president, or the directors. How easily the general wrath is lost in this maze! Public indignation meets a cuirass of divided responsibility that scatters a shock which would have stretched iniquity prone. Till the law lifted its mailed fist, how futile were the agitations against grade crossings, link couplers, and fenderless cars! Instead of playing hide-and-seek in the intricacies of the corporate structure, public opinion should strike right for the top. Let it mark the tactics of the Philadelphia mothers who, after vain appeal to underlings to put in a gate at a railroad crossing their children must make on the way to school, stormed the office of the president of the road.

The directors of a company ought to be individually accountable for every case of misconduct of which the company receives the benefit, for every preventable deficiency or abuse that regularly goes on in the course of the business. Hold them blameless if they prove the inefficiency or disobedience of underlings, but not if they plead ignorance. Consider the salutary side-effects of such severity. When an avalanche of wrath hangs over the head of the director of a sinning corporation, no one will accept a directorship who is not prepared to give a good deal of time and serious attention to its business. Strict accountability will send flying the figure-head directors who, when the misdeeds of their protégés come to light, protest they "did n't know." It will bar buccaneering insiders from using a group of eminent dummies as unwitting decoys for the confiding investor or policy-holder. It will break up the game of operating a brigand public-service company (owned by some distant "syndicate") from behind a board of respectable local "directors" without a shred of power.

Let it be understood that a man's reputation may be blasted by scandal within his corporation and we shall not see men directors on a score or two of boards. In New York City one man is found to be director of forty-five railroads, another of forty-two, others of thirty-seven, thirty-five, twenty-eight, twenty-two roads. Fifteen men are in sixteen or more railroads, thirty-four are directors of from ten to fifteen roads. Forty-eight are directors of seven roads or more. Those on the boards of from two to six roads are almost innumerable. Seventy-six men holding among them about sixteen hundred directorships are said, on high authority, to control fully one hundred of the greatest railroad, industrial, and banking corporations, with a capital equal to one fifth of the national wealth! Now, stricter accountability would greatly enlarge this directing *personnel* and perhaps rid it of some of that plutocratic arrogance which is inseparable from filling boards of directors with Wall Street bankers and speculators and a few men of enormous wealth. By enlisting more men with an interest in the technical side of the business, or in the community it serves, the evils of financial directorates would be mitigated.

In one state, newspapers have been required to print in every issue the name and place of business of the publisher or proprietor in order that the responsibility of the paper may be certain. It ought likewise to be customary to print along with the news of the exposure of corporation misconduct the names of the directors, in order that the public indignation may not explode without result, but find rather a proper target; for just indig-

nation is altogether too precious a thing
to be wasted.

Make it vain for a director to plead
that he opposed the wrong sanctioned by
the majority of his colleagues. If he will
keep his skirts clear, let him resign the
moment he is not ready to stand for every
policy of his board. In the board of directors, as in the cabinet of parliamentary
countries, the principle of joint responsibility should hold. It ought to be as inev-
itable for the entire board of directors of
a railroad company caught systematically
stealing mineral lands or oppressing coal
operators along its line, to resign, as now
it is a matter of course for college trustees
to resign when they have been caught
unloading bad securities on to the college
funds.

The trust practice of cross-checking,
setting off plant against plant, and one
department in a plant against corresponding departments in all the other plants,

while keying up technical efficiency, drives the superintendents and foremen under this staccato rivalry to bear hard on labor. The public conscience will not tolerate such ruthless exercise of corporate might, especially when the workers are women, or children, or unskilled. Let directors become habituated to full responsibility, and a reputable man will decline to stand for the treatment of labor under modern systems of cost accounting, unless he is protected by a " labor commissioner" or "welfare manager" responsible directly to a committee of the directors. It would be the duty of such an officer to limit the pressure of foremen on the workers, and to standardize at the level of the moral sentiment of the time such matters as hours, night-work, pay for overtime, safety provisions, accident indemnity, the conditions surrounding women and children, and the treatment of company customers or tenants.

Corporations are necessary, yet, through nobody's fault, they tend to become soulless and lawless. By all means let them reap where they have sown. But why let them declare dividends not only on their capital, but also on their power to starve out labor, to wear out litigants, to beat down small competitors, to master the market, to evade taxes, to get the free use of public property? Nothing but the curb of organized society can confine them to their own grist and keep them from grinding into dividends the stamina of children, the health of women, the lives of men, the purity of the ballot, the honor of public servants, and the supremacy of the laws.

VI

THE RULES OF THE GAME

THE RULES OF THE GAME

In the time when the family lived wholly off the produce of its own farm, questions of the distribution of wealth and of welfare could scarcely arise. But now that every man pours his product into some market, it enters in a way into social wealth and passes out of his control. What he shall have to show for it depends on factors which, as John Stuart Mill showed, are man-made rather than natural. He is obliged to enter a game, and to a degree his share of the Desirable depends on his success in that game. What hazards the game shall involve is largely within the will of organized society. Some temperaments want the risks great, the prizes big even if they must be few. Other temperaments want risk eliminated and something guaranteed for all. So long as both temperaments are present in society, it is safe to say that the game will be kept interesting by preserving something of risk. The establishment of the rules of the game lies within the province of society; and, seeing that the good or ill fortune of the player depends not only on his skill and means, but also on the rules of the game and how they are respected, it is worth while to consider the bearing on the social welfare of the various policies society may pursue.

THE NON-ENFORCEMENT OF THE RULES OF THE GAME RUPTURES AT LAST THE SOCIAL PEACE

According to Plato, when Socrates, on the morning of his last day, is urged by his friends to escape from prison, the philosopher refuses because in imagination he hears the Laws of Athens saying to him: "What do you mean by trying to escape but to destroy us, the Laws, and the whole city so far as in you lies? Do you think that a state can exist and not be overthrown in which the decisions of law are of no force and are disregarded and set at naught by private individuals?"

All failure to enforce law is bad, but in certain classes of law slackness is not so mischievous as it is in others. There is a group of laws aiming to restrain men from preying on the vices of their fellows and thereby weakening the physical and the moral fibre of the population. If saloon, dive, gambling den, betting ring, or pool-room bribe themselves free of these laws, they not only continue their work of ruin, but incidently the police is corrupted and, in a measure, all law is weakened.

Again, if the administration of justice becomes so feeble that the police cannot catch, nor the courts hang, the red slayer, the laws for the protection of persons become cobwebs and men resort freely to the personal redress of real or fancied wrongs. Murders and homicides would hardly be several times as frequent now as they were in 1880, but for the fact that in this country for years only one slayer out of seventy has been brought to the gallows. The harvest is bloodshed, lynching mobs, and race friction.

There is, however, another type of law-impotence which loosens the masonry of the state itself, and hence menaces the sober and orderly people who are beyond the reach of the lawlessness of "water-front," or "levee," or "tenderloin," or "Little Italy." This is failure to enforce the laws governing the conduct of groups or classes in their economic struggle, in a word, failure to uphold *the rules of the game*.

If the laws guarding the interests of one class are enforced, while the counterbalancing statutes protecting another class lie dormant, or if a law is enforced downward but not upward, or if Justice wields a sword on the poor but a lath on the rich and influential, the cheated class fiercely resolves to capture the state and to govern ruthlessly in its own interests. But, imbued with this vengeful spirit, government soon becomes the engine rather than the arbiter of conflicting interests, and the state sense perishes in the flame of class hate. This is why it may be more imperative to cut out alike Pinkertons and sluggers, to put down impartially corporation law-breaking and mob violence, than to enforce the ordinances for the "red light" district.

Suffering the big player to violate the rules of the game is doubly dangerous at the present stage. In twenty years two developments — the disappearance of free land in the rain belt, and the triumph of the big concern over the little — have narrowed the circle of opportunity for workingmen to achieve independence, and therefore tend powerfully to consolidate wage-earners into a conscious class. It does not yet appear whether this will make impossible that government by public opinion which has contributed so much to the good temper and steadiness of American society.

But there would remain government as compromise, and even on this lower plane the state may successfully guard the primary social interests. Not so, however, if hard-won political victory becomes a mockery because prosecutors are timid, or judges deferential, or executives suave, before the lusty law-breaker who is lord of the Desirable. "Jug-handled" administration of the laws kills the spirit of give-and-take, hardens the hearts of the outlawed class, and sets their jaws in the grim resolve to grasp the reins of power with a relentless hand and to retain them, if need be, by force.

The hustler's practice of "Get there — anyhow!" is warm sand for the hatching of cockatrice's eggs. In Pennsylvania the law-abiding disposition was so weakened by the Standard Oil Company's example that a man who tapped a pipe-line and stole Standard oil for two years was found innocent by jurors who had heard him plead guilty. In California the Southern Pacific Railroad Company brought law into such contempt that the train robbers, Evans and Sontag, were befriended by nearly the whole local population. In certain Rocky Mountain states mine operators and miners have both well-nigh lost the state sense, and reach for a judgeship or a sheriffalty as unhesitatingly as in a fight one would reach for a crowbar. Thus breach of law begets counter-breach. "Slush funds" and chicane soon breed mobs and terrorism, which in turn engender deportations, kidnappings, and brutal trampling upon the constitutional rights of citizens and communities. Brickbat, "acid egg," dynamite, and torch are in a way companion to "plum tree," "driftwood,"

gangster's gavel, and "bull pen." Nor
is it easy to revive the olive tree, once
the bramble has come up. It will take
years of even-handed enforcement of law
to restore to government in Colorado its
lost prestige. A decade of Solon and Rha-
damanthus cannot inspire the law-abiding
spirit that one year of weak government
or slack opinion can destroy. Hence the
question of how the game is played may
be more serious than the question of who
wins. A selfish interest that fights in the
open for the repeal of good laws is not to
be censured in the same breath with an
interest which seeks to chloroform these
same laws by packing a commission, or
"squaring" an inspector, or owning a
judge.

To be sure, clash of interest arises as we
leave behind the simple, homogeneous society of the early day; but it is not written
that every such conflict shall invade politics
and make the state its football. Knights

jousting in the mediæval tourney did not expect the keeper of the lists to enter the fray. An athletic team with the instinct of sportsmanship does not count on winning through the partiality of the umpire. Likewise farmers and middlemen, landlords and tenants, producers and consumers, manufacturers and mill-hands, single-line merchants and department stores, jostled together by circumstance, may fight with lawful weapons without laying hand to government. So long, indeed, as civic feeling is deep, the great majority of citizens shrink from using the state for the furtherance of their special group interests, and will not unite on such lines save to ward off the aggressions of some less scrupulous group.

The state inspires this reverence because it is felt to express our best selves. If happily constituted, it embodies our reason, fair-mindedness, and humaneness, not our passion, greed, and narrowness. This is why tax-payers will have their government build more solidly than they build themselves; why they will sanction in government sacrifices for a remoter posterity than they will sacrifice for individually; why they will not have their officers show in the punishment of criminals the vindictiveness, or in the treatment of dependents the parsimoniousness, they may feel in their own hearts.

Now, so long as battling groups feel that the law utters the best selves of their fellow citizens, they respect it, they hesitate to use it as an engine of their purposes. Moreover, they are content with the "square deal," because their dread of having the cards stacked against them prevails over the desire to stack them against others. But if government is weak or partial in upholding the rules of the struggle, or makes rules that favor one side as against the other, it forfeits this immunity. The arena of combat is shifted to politics. Impious hands are laid on the ark of the covenant. Into the law is injected now the greed of this class, now the vengefulness of that. As government thus degenerates, more and more expressing the common greed, hatred, and small-mindedness, instead of the common reason and conscience, it loses its power to command willing obedience, to conciliate jarring classes. This path leads to class war, and beyond that "the man on horseback."

TAMPERING WITH THE RULES OF THE GAME FINALLY BRINGS THE GAME ITSELF INTO DISCREDIT

Rules may be changed in the interest either of those about to enter the game, or of those actually in the game. The football code may be revised in order to benefit the sport, or in order to favor certain teams that happen to possess a star punter. So is it with changes in the laws. To be sure, they are made by men already in the game, —farmers, bankers, iron-moulders, etc., —

but these men in their policies may be thinking of themselves or thinking of their posterity. A man knows not what his sons will become and where their special interests will lie. So far, therefore, as they are concerned for their children, farmers, bankers, and iron-moulders can agree, and the changes they can agree on will be such as will make the social game fairer for all. Their laws will be righteous, and those who are hit by them cannot pose as victims of "class legislation." But when farmers or bankers or iron-moulders legislate for themselves as a class and to the damage of others, they pull the game askew and spoil it.

On considering how often in the last quarter century tariff-protected businesses, the railroads, the public utility corporations, telegraph, telephone, express, lumber, coal, oil, insurance, and the various trusts have captured and operated the machinery of government, one savors a fine irony in calling ours a régime of "individualism." Is it, then, a part of the game founded on private property and free enterprise to grant exclusive perpetual franchises, to exempt surplus values from taxation, to make the corporation charter a contract, to exalt corporations into citizens with a right to the enjoyment of interstate comity, to legitimate the holding company, to enjoin strikers from the exercise of fundamental rights, to debar a policy-holder from suing the management of an insurance company for an accounting, injunction, or receivership, save with the consent of the attorney-general of the state? Indeed, it would be easy to name commonwealths that exemplify nothing but the covert domination of Big Business. But it is impossible that men should long acquiesce in a régime of sheer capitalism. There is sure to form a body of tangent opinion denying everything that capitalism affirms and affirming everything that capitalism denies. The Nemesis of treating private property, freedom of en-

terprise, and corporate undertaking as instruments of *private gain* rather than of
public welfare, is the root-and-branch man
who urges us to escape the Unendurable by
taking refuge in the Impossible.

The revolutionary socialist charges to
" the competitive system " ills four fifths
of which arise from monopoly. He saddles
individualism with the sins of a commer-
cialized politics, and sees the polluter of
politics in capital rather than in Big Business. The abysmal inequalities of wealth
he deems a natural development under
"private ownership of the instruments of
production," rather than an outgrowth of
privilege. In swollen fortunes he sees the
vestibule not to plutocracy, but to social
revolution. Policies which protect the independent concerns and the petty properties he finds " reactionary." He stigmatizes
as " bourgeois " the endeavor to save the
little investors from the maw of the predatory financier, and dreams of a coming soci-

ety moulded to the heart's desire of wage-earners. Although, while rents and monopoly profits rise, the earnings of capital are falling, he proclaims the right of labor to the whole produce, and the wrongfulness of any return to the owner of capital. For a tested workable régime he offers a vague, ill-considered scheme built largely out of antitheses to the actual and sharply at variance with human nature on its present plane. Infatuated with his chimera, he lifts no finger to reach the near-by good, while his wild proposals excite apprehensions which hinder the progress of genuine constructive work.

The truth is, on the plane of our inherited institutions government might be so administered in the public-welfare spirit, that three fourths of the subversive sentiment existing would vanish. But the policy of "Score while you're in!" plays into the hands of the radicals who tell the workingman "there is no halfway house between capitalism and collectivism." "Our innings!" cries Big Business exultantly, and with fifty-year franchise laws, iniquitous tariff schedules, excessive railway-mail charges, grabbing of public mineral lands, corrupt sale of canals and gas plants, fake meat inspection, Niagara grabs, and the cynical denial of protection to labor, it plunges ahead, inviting the day when the cry will ring out, "To your tents, O Israel!" Every tampering with the simple logical rules of the game on the theory that if you take care of business business will take care of the general welfare, or if you take care of the capitalist the capitalist will take care of the workingman, adds to those who think the game itself so hopelessly bad that there is no use in trying to make it fair.

In the sphere of opinion nothing so favors the root-and-branch men as the ascendency of commercial standards of success. Certainly you may rate the business man by the money he has been able to make under the rules of his game. But the sages of all time agree that the writer, thinker, scholar, clergyman, jurist, officer, administrator, and statesman must not be mere profit seekers, nor may their social standing depend on their financial rating. The intrusion of Mammon's standards into such callings makes socialists of thousands who do not really believe that the exchange of money for labor is " exploitation."

Those who put their faith in a transfigured individualism should make haste to clean the hull of the old ship for the coming great battle with the opponents of private capital and individual initiative. Certainly many of the villainies and oppressions that befoul it are no more a part of individualism than are the barnacles and trailing weed a part of the vessel. Moreover, if they are to put up a good fight for the ship, it behooves them to rid it of the buccaneers, wreckers, and shanghaiers that now impudently claim the shelter of its flag, and by their sinister presence compromise the efforts of its legitimate defenders.

THE CONSPICUOUSLY SUCCESSFUL VIOLATER
OF THE RULES OF THE GAME ROBS US
OF THAT WHICH IS MORE PRECIOUS
THAN GOLD

The enterprises that have succeeded by trampling on the laws have done worse than extort money from us. After all, the monopolist as such hurts us no more than a drouth, a May frost, the boll weevil, or the chinch bug; and these are not calamities of the first rank, for, though they lessen our comfort, they do not leave us less civilized. But as successful law-breaker, the monopolist takes from us more than money: he takes away our ideals, leaving us more ape and less man. For twenty years the writer has watched the effect upon college young men of the conspicuous triumph of the first great commercial pirate — the oil trust —

over able competitors, common carriers, oil producers, public prosecutors, attorneys-general, courts, legislatures, newspapers, and leaders of opinion. Many left college for the battle of life with the conviction that the ideals of success held up by their instructors were unpractical. "The preachers and professors and commencement speakers are old fogies," says one. "This is n't the kind of world they think it is. They are fussy old maids, not strong men." "With all these fine principles," says another, "you'd be a dead one from the start. You'd never get into the game at all." "Money's the thing! With money you're It, no matter who kicks," says a third. "I'm going to climb into the band-wagon, not hoot at it as it goes by." So, for several college generations, one could mark in the ebb of generous ideals and the mounting of a precocious cynicism the working of the virus. If such was the impression of triumphant lawlessness upon young men whose horizon had been widened by academic culture, what must it have been upon the multitudes of callow youth that from the school-boy desk go ill-furnished forth into active life? The founder of the oil trust may give us back our money, but not if he send among us a hundred Wesleys can he give us back the lost ideals.

UNLESS RULES BE ENFORCED, THE MORAL PLANE WILL NOT BE LIFTED SIMPLY BY ADDING TO THE NUMBER OF RIGHTEOUS MEN

Many spiritual leaders imagine that the Kingdom of Heaven comes simply by regenerating souls, that as man after man turns his face upward society is duly uplifted. It would follow that the quiet work on individuals does not need to be supplemented by the recourse to law or public opinion, and that the Puritan's endeavor to *establish righteousness* is superfluous.

This may have been true before competition became lord of life, but now that the few lead off while the rest must follow suit, much depends on giving the lead to the good man rather than the bad man. You may add to the number of good men, but, without enforced rules, it will be impossible for them to stay in the higher posts and callings. For the social trend denies most men a free hand. More and more the chief vocations come under the baton of competition, so that one may not maintain one's self in them at all unless one feels at liberty to do as his rivals are permitted to do. Those in the same line must move in lock step, and the pace is set by the meanest man who is allowed to continue in the business. The department store that pays its girls living wages and closes at six can hardly live in the same town with one that pays four dollars a week and closes at nine. If the price of glass jars is fixed by the manufacturer who overdrives little boys, every competitor must, unless he possesses some offsetting advantage, conform to this practice. Leave the business he may, change it he cannot. If one dealer in foods successfully adulterates, his fellows must follow suit or else seek their patrons among the few who prefer a brand because it is dear. As for the dispenser of pure drugs, there is no place for him until the law steps in to standardize quality. The one shipper who extorts an illegal rate obliges all other shippers in his line to break the law or be snuffed out. So long as there are able attorneys willing to handle the corporation work just as it comes, clean or dirty, the lawyer who insists on picking and choosing must mildew in the basement of his profession. If the lavish use of money is countenanced in politics, no poor man can win without truckling to the contributors of campaign funds.

It is chiefly the directive groups in the social scale that are thus swayed by the twentieth man. The privates in the indus-

trial army do not move in lock step, for
they keep step with their officer ; their per-
formance is standardized for them by those
who give out the work. Farmers are independent, and on the soil a man may still
live up to his ideals. In the learned pro-
fessions there are tricks, to be sure, but the
quack cannot set the pace. But in business,
finance, and politics it is more and more
the case that all who maintain themselves
therein must stand on about the same foot-
ing. Without pressure from outside, the
moral level of practice will be low, and the
good man will have to stagnate or get out.
The rule of money in politics means
" Wear the collar or quit." The control of
the press by financial interests is a placard,
" Stubborn truth-tellers not wanted." The
reckless rivalry among life insurance companies advertises, " No room for the con-
servative manager." If it becomes common
for dealers to give " commissions " to servants or purchasing agents, the sign might

as well be hung out, " No one who will not bribe need apply."

How vain, then, to expect to better conditions simply by adding to the number of good men ! The converts would be obliged to join the multitudes who have their work cut out for them. They might, of course, hew coal or lay bricks or drive oxen. But business, finance, and politics and journalism — so potent in the allotment of wealth and of welfare, so authoritative in impressing standards on the rising generation — would become no whit better. There are already enough granite men to man the high posts; but, till the ways be cleared for them, they accumulate on the lower levels where, having no free hand, they feel no moral responsibility. By themselves they can get no foothold at the strategic points where conditions are made, where the weal or woe of thousands is determined. Without aid they cannot maintain themselves in these competitive fields. It is, therefore, the first duty of society *to establish the righteous by lifting the plane of competition.*

Pure food laws mean an open door for honest men in the purveying business. An efficient state insurance department means a chance for the " old-fashioned" manager. A stricter ethical code for the legal profession would enable certain briefless lawyers to forge to the front. Child-labor restriction is a godsend to the humane manufacturer. Outlawing the sweaters' dens may throw the ready-made clothing trade into the hands of reputable men. Already in banking we see a business, once the happy hunting ground of swindlers, which, by regulation, has come to be a field for honorable men.

It is easy to see what fifty years of public condemnation of liquor-selling has done in driving good men out of it. It is easy to foresee what a lively public appreciation and support of truth-telling newspapers, of plain-spoken preachers, of fearless scholars, of civic-minded lawyers, of conscientious merchants, of humane manufacturers, of upright officials, of zealous prosecutors, would do to populate these walks with good men.

How useless is character without opportunity can be read in our recent political history. In growing numbers during the late eighties and the nineties, party machines, lackey to the greedy interests, strove to retire from politics men of high ideals and independent spirit. If, during his trial term, the popular district attorney, mayor, legislator, or congressman spurned the collar, at the end a hidden trap-door fell, and he dropped to oblivion. If the ringsters could not scheme or slander or gavel him down in the nominating convention, they knifed him at the polls. Oiled by corporation money the machines did their work well, and the resulting survival of the pliable added steadily to the putty faces in public life.

Wiseacres laid the conspicuous decline in public men to general moral decay or to the superior attractions of the business career, blind to the like falling off in the character of the business men of the period, and unaware that the bulk of the American people are as rich as ever in red corpuscles. That the spinal sort found politics full of blocked stairways, while the gutta-percha manikins of the bosses and the Big Men of the Interests were carried smoothly upward in the party elevator, brought about, at last, that mortifying end-of-the-century situation when, over perhaps a third of the country, the upper floors of the political fabric showed a dwindling contingent of bold and public-spirited men. From the upward rush of sterling characters in the five years since the grip of the " organization " began to be loosened and the political stairways cleared, judge what we lost during the decades when we let so many consciences knock vainly at the barred portals of public life!

Some, alive to the pace-setting power of the twentieth man, stigmatize competition as deteriorating and cry out that it is idle to expect improvement until the competitive system is abolished. This would be pouring out the baby with the bath. Competition may pursue an upward path or a downward path. When makers adulterate or lyingly advertise, or overdrive their help, or replace men with children, they follow the downward path. When they eliminate waste, improve their processes, utilize by-products, install better machines, they follow the upward path. Collective industry would avoid the downward path, but it might not follow the upward path. The true policy is to fence off the downward paths and leave competition free to spur rivals into the upward path.

THE RESISTANCE TO THE ENFORCEMENT OF RIGHTEOUS RULES CONSTANTLY INCREASES

Restraint breeds a resistance corresponding to the loss it imposes. When we go to short-chain the interests which prey on men's vices, they snap at us like jackals. Collective ownership of public utilities may quiet the special interests that now rage in the halter of regulation, but by the time their anti-civic career is ended another range of enterprises will be springing against the leash. We declare pipe-lines common carriers with the duty to file tariffs, and we get refusal, subterfuges, freak tariffs, and onerous requirements that bar independents from using the lines. If our children will not be called upon to fix gas prices and street car fares in the teeth of concentrated private interest, they will have their hands full in regulating railroad, telegraph, express, in-

surance, pipe-line, and news-service rates;
wharf, dock, storage, and cotton-baling
charges; the prices of oil, anthracite coal,
ice, and school books; and in prescribing
the conditions of manufacture and sale
of articles all the way from dressed beef
to corporation securities.

Every year the points of contact—and
of friction—between government and private
interests have multiplied. In the days
of well-water, candles, sorghum, and flat
boats, there were no water, gas, sugar, or
railroad interests to vex politics. Home-
grown food did not call for the inspector.
Till the factory came there was no need
to bar children from toil or to enforce the
guarding of dangerous machinery. A generation ago the little razor-back gas and
horse-car companies had no call to mix
in politics; but the advent of water-gas
and the trolley, coupled with urban growth,
gave them the lard of monopoly profit to
defend, and made the public-service cor-

porations the arch-corrupters of city councils. Once the railroads competed, but their consolidators have driven the despairing shipper to look to government for protection. On all sides we see businesses that, feeling less and less the automatic curb of competition, will soon need the snaffle of public regulation.

As the smoke lifts we can mark just who are resisting law and corrupting government. In the cities the fight is chiefly with the vice-caterers and the public-service corporations. The former want a "wide open" town. The latter want unhampered enjoyment of their monopoly power. They are law-defying until they own the source of law and can get perpetual grants on easy terms with a free hand as to prices and fares and exemption of their franchise values from taxation. Battling along with these big interests are bankers scheming for deposits of city funds, rookery landlords in terror of the health-officer, business men intent on grabbing an alley or a water-front, and contractors eager to "job" public works.

The state government labors heavily like a steamboat working through the *sudd* on the Upper Nile. The railroads want to avert rate regulation and to own the state board of equalization. The gas and street-railway companies want "ripper" legislation, the authorization of fifty-year franchises, and immunity from taxation of franchises or limitation of stock-watering. Manufacturers want the unrestricted use of child labor. Mining companies dread short-hour legislation. Publishers want their text-books foisted upon the schools. The baking-powder trust wants rival powders outlawed. The oil trust wants to turn safety inspection against the independents. A horde of harpies have the knife out for pure-food bills. Brewers, distillers, elevator combines, pet banks, rotten insurance companies — all have a motive for undermining government by the people.

Thus time adds to the number of interests intent to break or to skew the rules of the game. The phalanx lengthens of those who want government to be of india rubber and not of iron. Of course this resistance produces results. Under a pressure of ten talents men collapse who were adamant under the pressure a single talent can exert. In view of the temptations we send them against, we ought not to marvel that so many public servants bend or break. It is not to be expected that government can withstand the growing strain without many structural improvements. In any case, it is certain that to the upholding of the rules of the game society must devote an increasing share of its thought and conscience.